THE JOURNAL PROJECT
DIALOGUES AND CONVERSATIONS
INSIDE WOMEN'S STUDIES

The Journal Project

DIALOGUES AND CONVERSATIONS
INSIDE WOMEN'S STUDIES

EDITED BY
DANA PUTNAM, DOROTHY KIDD,
ELAINE DORNAN, PATTY MOORE

CANADIAN CATALOGUING IN PUBLICATION DATA

Main entry under title:
The journal project: dialogues and conversations inside women's studies

ISBN 0-929005-69-4

1. Women. 2. Women - Social conditions.
3. Women college students - British Columbia - Vancouver.
I. Putnam, Dana.

HQ1154.J68 1995   305.4   C95-931030-4

Edited by Beverley Beetham Endersby
Copyedited by Debbie Viets
Cover art and illustrations by Mia Tremblay

Second Story Press gratefully acknowledges the assistance
of The Canada Council and the Ontario Arts Council.

Printed and bound in Canada

Published by
SECOND STORY PRESS
720 Bathurst Street, Suite 301
Toronto, Canada
M5S 2R4

CONTENTS

INTRODUCTION
9

CHAPTER ONE
BEGINNING WOMEN'S STUDIES
Introduction *25*
First Impressions *27*
Holding Forth *40*

CHAPTER TWO
NAMING
Introduction *51*
Who and What is "Family" *53*
Body and Imaging *80*
Sexuality *96*
Violence Against Women *120*

CHAPTER THREE
WARNING: FEMINIST CONTENT TO FOLLOW
Introduction *143*
Site: Women's Studies *145*
Changing the Terms *166*

CHAPTER FOUR
BRINGING IT HOME
Introduction *179*

CHAPTER FIVE
AFTERWORDS
201

CONTRIBUTORS' NOTES
214

BIBLIOGRAPHY
221

ACKNOWLEDGEMENTS

COLLECTIVELY, WE HAVE a long list of people to thank. Cynthia Flood, Penny Goldsmith, Janisse Browning, Frances Wasserlein, Mac Nelson and Jana Williams for their advice and support; Jean Burgess for originating journals in the Women's Studies program at Langara, and Michaelah Fox and Kate Slaney for helping to get this project started; the women at Second Story Press for all their support and hard work; and the five anonymous reviewers for their helpful advice. Although we cannot name them all here, we would like to acknowledge the many people who provided us with instrumental advice and encouragement over the past three years.

We would especially like to thank all of the contributors who assisted in the preparation of the manuscript for this book, including Margaret Sutherland and Joanna Pearson for typing and transcribing; Coral Gallagher for phoning; Terry Gibson for her editorial support; Darcian Welychenko and Julie Archer for their library research on the bibliography; Morgan Brayton, Women's Centre liaison, for her emotional support; and the Langara Women's Centre Collective and Langara Student Union for their financial support. And all the students and instructors in Langara's Women's Studies program who have challenged us in so many ways.

Dana would like to "name my daughter, Sylvia, my partner Dan, my mom, Lona, and my good friends Kim Smith and Elaine Dornan, all of whom have encouraged and supported me while I was working on this project."

Dorothy would like to thank Margaret Easto Kidd, Penny Goldsmith, Cisco, Terry Gibson and Denise Nadeau for their constant supply of ideas and encouragement.

Elaine would like to thank "my daughters, Adrienne and Ashley, for their insights, support and energy. My thanks to Roger Holdstock, who, as my first college instructor, was instrumental in my choice to continue in school and who repeatedly recommended I take Women's Studies — great advice!"

Patty would like to thank "my daughter, Katie, for being herself; my mom and dad, Dorothy and Jim Moore, for leaving me with a legacy of believing challenges are worth meeting; and many friends and co-workers who have given inspiration to this book and to my teaching."

Finally, our deepest gratitude to all the contributors who entrusted their personal thoughts to *The Journal Project*.

INTRODUCTION

I KEEP A JOURNAL and often take time to write in one of Vancouver's many cafés, restaurants or parks. I am seldom alone — the city must be home to thousands of journal writers, most of whom are women. Among the many media of expression that women have been seizing, it is perhaps the most affordable. With only a notebook and a pen, and the time for an extended coffee break, many of us are now taking the nooks and crannies of public space to make "rooms of our own." And while contemporary women's journal writing is an extension of the diary or personal letter of women of earlier generations, many women now use the medium, as Virginia Woolf first espoused, to birth thoughts and feelings long denied in public discourse (Woolf, 1945).

In June 1994, a number of this book's contributors got together for a series of discussions about their use of journals and the value of journal writing inside and outside the classroom. (A version of this discussion is included in Chapter Five.) Several began by remembering the plastic-covered diaries with tiny lock and keys that they had kept as young girls. Most had continued to write in some kind of diary or journal as they got older, using it as a private space to bring to life some of their most intimate feelings and thoughts.

Many felt they didn't have anyone else to talk to. For Leah, her journal was the only place she had in which to say anything. For Terry, her journal was the only means of communication during two years in which she didn't speak. Both Debbra and Sima took their diaries to bed with them at night: Debbra described hers as a friend, "someone who would always be there," while Sima described hers as a lover, to whom she could "say everything" and not have to "hide any part of me."

The forms their writing took ranged from letters to mono-
logues, to poetry and short stories. Many, such as Laura, wrote only
during times of great transitions. Others would write when they
were confused, or to sort things out. As Debbra said:

> When I was little there used to be a point where I couldn't go to
> bed at night until I'd written 'cause I was so — I don't know —
> words are really awkward for me and writing on paper has
> always been very safe.... If I'm having a hard time with some-
> thing and I do write, I can feel the difference in the situation,
> like it's less stress. I'm more kind of in tune with myself.... I
> really enjoy writing and I find that it's really therapeutic.

And Daphne:

> I'm very nervous talking to people, and I guess that's why I've
> kept journals on and off for a very long time, because I always
> felt that when I talked to people I would never get the true
> sense of who I was. I always preferred how I sounded when I
> read what I'd written. It just makes more sense. My personality,
> when it's down on paper, is tangible.

BEGINNING THE COLLECTION

This volume of journal writing emerged from the Women's Studies
Program at Langara College in Vancouver, British Columbia. We
began to collect the material in 1992 as the result of a joint initiative
of students and teachers. As one of the co-editors, Dana Putnam,
recalls:

> Halfway through my first Women's Studies class, I realized that
> some of the most important stuff was getting put down in my
> journal. At first I felt that I was the only one going through this
> really heavy stuff, but soon realized others were too. And I want-
> ed access to how the other women in the class were coping.
>
> I didn't think it was fair that only the instructors got to see
> the journals. There wasn't enough time in class to discuss many
> of the issues in any depth and I wanted to hear what the other
> women really thought. So I began to talk to others and we all
> felt that it would be great if we could read each other's journals.

At the same time as Dana Putnam was talking to her classmates, Patty Moore and I were discussing how to share some of the writing we were reading as Women's Studies teachers. Each week when we'd take an armful of notebooks home to read, I would feel I was privy to some very important "stuff." I was often stilled with sadness at the stories being told or by the clarity of thought or feeling. Patty and I would regularly talk about the fresh insights expressed by women who were connecting their own experiences to the perspectives and analyses we were discussing in the course.

We came together out of those two parallel conversations to compile this collection. Three years later, the editorial group comprises two students and two teachers, and several student and teacher volunteers who perform specific tasks. As with many other feminist projects, we have tried to work with our differences in vision, skills and experience, ever conscious of one another's commitments to children, school and other paid and unpaid community projects. Our combined experience as students and teachers has given us, as Elaine has said, "a real strength that has been instrumental in our ability to improvise and work with the challenges that continue to arise." In a recent discussion, Dana and Elaine suggested that, "while we never explicitly discussed the traditional power imbalance between students and teachers, we seem to implicitly have shifted towards a healthier and more egalitarian group dynamic."

We decided to publish the work for several reasons. Dana commented:

> I didn't really know what I was supposed to be doing when I was asked to do a journal. I thought what we could do would be to show all the different ways journals were being done, not like a model, but to give students several examples to help them get started.

Elaine remarked:

> My journals were a place I could work on ideas and emotions, giving me the confidence to ask some of the really hard questions. When I became involved in this project it was an inspiration for me to find out what other women's reactions were, to know that it wasn't just me thinking these things. I thought a book would allow me to take their comments and respond in my own way.

Patty said:

We wanted to give students examples, to show how other women have worked at the same assignment.... One of our goals in Women's Studies is to encourage women to reflect, to look at the new information they are learning in light of their own experience and values.

LOCATING OUR PROJECT

All of us agreed that it was important to document both the journal writing process and the content of what women were writing. I was continually shocked and inspired to read again and again how women were still experiencing and challenging many of the same daily conditions — violence in the home and outside, poverty, racism, heterosexism — that had propelled me twenty years earlier to get involved in the women's movement. There was also a rawness and vibrancy in the writing that mocked the myth that contemporary women have no need for women's movements. We all thought that the value of journal writing, and of the issues and ideas that women were bringing to these pages, was not limited to our college on the west coast of Canada.

As we discovered the large numbers of people and programs using journal writing, and the growing controversy about their use within Women's Studies, we realized how important it was to describe the very particular context in which we as students and instructors produce this work. As part of Langara College, the Women's Studies Program draws from a wide cross-section of Vancouver's population. (During a recent strike, it was reported that fully one-twelfth of Vancouver residents have attended the school at some time.) The Women's Studies Program itself was born in the heady days of 1970s feminism and we still emphasize our women's movement origins, underscoring grass-roots activism in the hiring of instructors; in course design, content and teaching methods; and in complementary film and lecture series.

The program offers two introductory courses and two second-year courses — on Women and Sexuality and Women and Social Change — for classes of twenty to thirty-five students, most of whom are women. Through guest speakers, group projects and fieldwork assignments, we encourage students to apply the experience and connections they have brought with them, or to find new ground for working together with others at the college and with organizations in the wider community. I am regularly reminded of the way the program is fed by, and, in turn, feeds the larger women's movements: not a week goes by that I do not meet an ex-student at a community meeting, event, demonstration or cultural performance, or staffing a women's organization.

Journals are one way that students are encouraged to reflect on the life experience they bring to the class. Unlike the practice in many other programs, the journals are completion assignments and are not graded. Four to five times a semester journal entries on topics chosen by the student, not prompted by instructors, are submitted. The instructor's response is intended to encourage students to keep writing in the first person, and to reflect on what they bring from their own values and experiences to their process of learning and construction of meaning. Elaine describes the journal's value as providing "a safer space for dialogue with myself and the instructor"; for Dana, journals provide a place where "we can say things that there isn't time, space or safety to say in class."

In part, as a consequence of both our community orientation and the heterogeneous composition of the college, women choose to write about a number of different issues, from a wide base of life experience. Ranging in age from eighteen to sixty-five, back to school after thirty years' absence, or on their way to university directly from high school, contributors had taken at least one, and perhaps up to four, of our courses. From many different family and cultural backgrounds, the contributors currently live in a variety of heterosexual, lesbian and bisexual households.

Many had kept diaries before: however, few had thought of themselves as writers, and fewer still had ever been published. While some were long-time activists from a variety of social movements, most were new to feminism, or to critical social analysis of any kind. The pieces range from testimonials to essays to poetry. None was written for publication; all were solicited and submitted after the completion of the semester in which the piece was written.

NEW IDENTITIES AND NEW LITERARY FORMS

While compiling this collection, we read several commentaries by contemporary writers who have also valued the potential of journal writing as a social and political act (see Bibliography). These included teachers such as Elouise Bell (1985), who noted that "everyone has a story to tell." However, while women have almost always written, they have seldom been published. Another instructor, Susan Waugh (1985), describes how

> writing and reading about the lives of "ordinary people" can be occasions for learning and teaching, for imagining a better world, for respect and love. Autobiographical writings can also be forges in which new identities and new literary forms are shaped (152).

Critics have also commented on the role of autobiographical writing in oppositional social movements. For bell hooks (1989), diary-keeping has had a special place in female experience, as

> a writing act that intimately connects the art of expressing one's feeling on the written page with the construction of self and identity, with the effort to be fully self-actualized.... [It] has been crucial to women's development of a counter-hegemonic experience of creativity within patriarchal culture.... In many cases where such writing has enhanced our struggle to be self-defining, it emerges as a narrative of resistance, as writing which enables us to experience both self-discovery and self-recovery (72).

In a similar vein, Nancy Saporta Sternbach (1991) has commented on the tradition of testimonials in Latin America, noting the importance of retrieving, reconstructing and recovering women's history in the development of a "new consciousness as political subjects" (92).

With the recognition of their importance, journals have increasingly come into use within formal and non-formal education. Many teachers of Women's Studies, English as a primary and secondary language, basic literacy and other social science and humanities courses now use some form of journal assignment. These vary widely, from journals such as ours that are not graded, with topics chosen by each student, to graded commentaries on course material such as readings or presentations.

Many teachers have adopted an approach similar to ours and use the journal as a tool for critical thinking and self-evaluation. Journal keeping can encourage students to recognize, appreciate and reflect upon their personal interpretations, helping them develop an awareness of how meaning is constructed (Wollman-Bonilla, 1989). Duke (cited in Zacharias, 1991) notes their use in aiding students in decision making, encouraging them to discuss controversy, committing themselves fully to positions and becoming autonomous thinkers. "It is a means — perhaps the best means — to make knowledge personal, connected and accessible to the self" (Strong, cited in Zacharias, 266).

DEALING WITH THE MESSINESS: CONTROVERSY OR REASSESSMENT?

As journal keeping as a classroom assignment has become more prevalent, a controversial reassessment is being made of their use and value, particularly within Women's Studies programs. Keith Louise Fulton (1992), for example, has written about the need to consider "power differentials and ethical guidelines for conduct" in using journals in academic institutions. In most colleges and universities, where more power resides with the instructor, and where the authority of academic discourse still largely undervalues Women's Studies and women's autobiographical writing, Fulton says "the journal then becomes either an extensive writing project directed to another person, or writing performed as though it were confidential when it is not" (430).

Ellen Berry and Elizabeth Black (1993) have suggested modifying journal writing and creating another kind of assignment, intended to transcend both the "true confessions" of their students' journals and the "cold knowledge of traditional academic discourse."

In the Women's Studies Program at Langara College, the four instructors have often discussed these problems. We recognize that, like "safe" sex, the safety that we can provide in journals cannot be absolute. We try to acknowledge both the social power we all have as instructors and also that some women might respond to each of us differently because of our individual identities as white or Black, lesbian or heterosexual, younger or older women. As instructors, we have encountered the stickiest situations when we have acted as readers of personal confessions or, even more problematically, of the expressions of racism, classism or homophobia.

Patty Moore suggests that the "messiness" of journal writing may well be inherent in the blending of personal voice and experience with social analysis, in an institutional setting. As teachers, we have chosen to not back away from the complexity of the problem, but rather have experimented with different kinds of journal-writing assignments and with different ways of responding that can be both supportive and useful for learning.

ANOTHER CONTROVERSY :
INCLUSION IN THE COLLECTION PROCESS

The editorial group decided to explore the controversy about the use of journals in Women's Studies classrooms in a dialogue with contributors (see Chapter Five). Long before reading some of the recent commentaries, we had become familiar with how power differences between women can literally line up on the page. Contributing a piece to this volume was voluntary, and in the first round of submissions we noticed some serious gaps in who and what was included. Initially, we received many fewer entries expressing the point of view of women of colour and/or immigrant women, fewer still from that of lesbians and almost none from the perspective of poor or working-class women. As a result, we attempted to widen the representation and to evaluate the composition of our editorial group — while almost all of us are mothers, some working class and/or poor, and some lesbian, none of us is a woman of the First Nations or of colour. This evaluation also pushed the two instructors to reassess course content and classroom practice. In the succeeding rounds of submissions, we encouraged more women to submit pieces that spoke from these experiences.

In the process, we came to better appreciate how risky it still is to write, and more specifically to submit for publication, from the perspectives of women not usually represented by the dominant culture. This very large group also includes women who are survivors of violence, and past or present sex-trade workers. In the end, we have tried to ensure that the collection is representative of a diversity of women writing about a wide number of concerns and not just about the specific components of their identity that they see as the most targeted and/or vulnerable.

In our classrooms, we discuss feminist perspectives on social location, emphasizing the importance of speaking for oneself, naming one's identities and issues. The choice offered contributors of using their own names or a pseudonym, or remaining wholly anonymous, has made this issue even more complicated, as one of the obvious markers of difference may be absent. As a result, while biographical notes on contributors are provided at the end of this book, we want to issue a caution to the reader: be aware of the assumptions you make. You may not know much about the identity of a contributor, whether she's of First Nations, European, Asian, African or mixed heritage; lesbian or heterosexual; living with a chronic illness; a sex-trade worker; or a member of any group with a visible or non-visible characteristic.

THE FRAMEWORK

This collection includes entries from a cross-section of the women enrolled in our classes during the last five years. Many entries fell very easily into thematic groupings. However, no section says it all; there are still several gaps in representation and perspective, and much that is still unsaid. It will not give you a definitive idea of what Women, with a capital W, are thinking today.

There are many other books available that provide that kind of account, detailing different women's perspectives on a wide range of specific issues. Other books tell readers how to write journals. Our aim is to combine elements from both genres: to demonstrate some of the ways that women use journals as instruments to name and make sense of their own everyday experience and of the women and men and larger world around them.

What you'll see in the following pages is the raw material from the journals of more than fifty women. The individual entries often sound like conversations. Our challenge has been twofold: to maintain the integrity of each piece and allow each woman to speak clearly and to show the richness of connection and variation among and between women. To do this, we have kept the copy-editing to a minimum, retaining some of the idiosyncrasies of spelling and punctuation. All of the introductions to the pieces were written later, when each contributor was asked to provide her own brief introduction to her entry or entries; nothing else substantive has been added.

As an editorial group we've played with the order of pieces, organizing them by subject matter within sections and chapters, and also by the rhythm and tenor of their expression. As these conversations are often intimate and can be intellectually and emotionally challenging, we have included introductions to each section, to provide some background in climate and context. Keeping with our general rule that each of us must speak only for herself, the co-editor who wrote each section introduction is identified.

Our first draft not only grouped the pieces thematically but also tried to suggest movement from individual reflection and naming to collective action, ending with future visions. However, we realized that we were imposing a rigidity on pieces and thinking processes that were still in flux. Our framework now is less linear and grew organically out of the submissions themselves. The collection begins with women's first reactions to Women's Studies and to journal writing, then progresses through women's locating of their personal identity issues to their experience as students in the Women's Studies Program or in other aspects of their lives. Finally, we include a partial transcript of a discussion among some of the contributors of journal writing and the project.

In Chapter One, Beginning Women's Studies, the contributors relate their first impressions of Women's Studies, an experience one woman describes as having "a door opened," another as looking at things in entirely new ways, or beginning to ask questions for which there are no ready-made answers. Several also discuss the reactions they got from old friends and family to news of their "discovery" of Women's Studies.

The other theme of this chapter is Holding Forth, in which women reflect on the uses they make of writing. A number note how early influences from family and school continue to have a grip on them, keeping their internal censors very powerful. Others discuss how they are learning to use their journals as places to note their sadness and anger, or as friends, or as the first steps towards speaking out loud.

The second chapter, Naming, focuses on themes of personal identity: Who and What Is Family? Body and Imaging, Sexuality, and Violence Against Women. Each entry documents the impact of these larger forces on the individual's make-up. Taken together, the entries in each section form a rich mosaic of women's experience. For example, while each contributor who writes about family relates the significance of her own individual family, the section as a whole gives us a very clear reminder of just how broad the meaning of "family" is today in Canada.

The three other themes in Chapter Two — Body, Sexuality and Violence against Women — form a triangle of female experience. Individual entries document women's experiences of their physicality, and their accounts of how that experience was shaped, and often mangled, by close and distant forces in the larger society. Together these three sections show the dynamics of women's continuing resistance to external pressures and violence, and their gradual reclamation of their bodies and sexualities.

Chapter Three, Warning: Feminist Content to Follow, contains two major themes. Site: Women's Studies is about the Women's Studies classroom and the larger college environment. Our school, like many other educational institutions, has become a site where women have converged, hungry to apply what they already know and to learn more. They write of the ways their points of view have shifted and how their beliefs have been challenged, reaffirmed or altered. They also write about those difficult moments when they have realized that "we" who have been told we are equal are not all the same. Speaking out from subject positions as women, and specifically as mothers, older women, women of colour, First Nations women, lesbians and sex-trade workers, can feel like a constant battle. The second section Changing the Terms, documents some of the reflections contributors have had after speaking out.

In Chapter Four, Bringing It Home, women write of the ways they are integrating their new learning with their lives outside the classroom, at home, in their paid work and in their community activities and organizing.

Chapter Five, Afterwords, shifts the perspective from solo voice to chorus. In June 1994, we convened a series of meetings with contributors and asked them what the process of journal writing had meant to them.

Most contributors felt that the Women's Studies journals had a different quality from their earlier diaries. For one thing, under severe time pressures, as Karen, balancing both studenthood and motherhood, said, "they created the space and time for me to write because I wouldn't have done it otherwise." Laura commented that her journal-writing experience fostered trust in "feminists working for change [and] in myself. Not because I was a brilliant scholar or philosopher, but because I am me."

Many said that they had, much more so than in their earlier diaries, used their journals to question everything they were learning, and to challenge themselves, both emotionally and intellectually. Leah used each entry as an opportunity to write about a specific topic and said that the experience was beneficial "in that I got a voice but I also was learning. So it actually did more for me than just personal writing. It made me look at issues that I might either avoid or just didn't know existed."

Margaret commented:

Women's Studies has been my sum total of post-secondary education and I haven't been able to continue with it. I've always been deeply ashamed of being uneducated. In my job as a secretary, you can imagine how many decisions I get to make and how many judgements I get to produce, and who cares what I think.... I haven't been able to continue with any more courses, but I don't think it's a coincidence that, during the time that I was concentrating hard on writing the journal, it felt like I was moving into a whole additional level of responsibility and authority within my life. My god, I may be qualified to have an opinion.

Several had experienced betrayal with earlier journals, the privacy of their writing having been violated by brothers or sisters, mothers or other guardians, and, as they grew older, by lovers. After such a betrayal, Sima had

decided to never again write my feelings on paper, and I didn't do it for years ... the first time that I did was in my Women's Studies course and I had to struggle with myself so much to let things come out. But then I found it very interesting, I loved the comments. Now whenever I write, I just want to give it to someone to read!

All the contributors said that they were very conscious of writing to another person, an instructor. For Debbra, "being in a Women's Studies class and also writing in the journal was like finally finding somebody to walk with after going through my whole life always feeling I was different." Leah compared this dialogue quality of journals to women writing letters to one another, a practice that was widespread in the nineteenth and early twentieth centuries in this country. Several other women described a more spiral type of communication where they spoke, with both their earlier selves and the instructor, about what they were learning.

In her written submission for the book, Terry talked about how valuable the experience had been, and that she believes that journals can assist "in guiding women to autonomy." She also acknowledged that her trust in the process had sometimes wavered: she was concerned about whether the instructors were able to handle any of the serious emotional crises that might be presented. For her, sometimes the replies were more like bandages "very skillfully placed over the wounds ... (using) mildly mirrored formula."

Terry raised concerns that many other students and teachers have voiced, as the use of journal writing in classrooms has grown exponentially. We asked participants to respond to some of the problems that can arise when journal assignments are institutionalized, used in formal settings where instructors maintain a great deal of power over students. What did they think about the idea that the encouragement of students' "authentic voice" in journal writing might be little more than a new technique for shaping women's thoughts and discourse? In Afterwords, contributors discuss this issue in more detail. For now, the last word is Margaret's:

> It was a contract kind of thing between teacher and student....
> I felt that if it was okay for me to hand in either as finely crafted a piece of work as I could possibly sweat out in two weeks, or something else that I wrote five minutes before the class

started, that I was going to allow the instructor the same privilege....

Perhaps I flatter myself, but I figure I had just as much of a chance of influencing the instructor as vice versa.... I really felt it was a correspondence.

— *DOROTHY*

Chapter One

BEGINNING
WOMEN'S
STUDIES

BEGINNING
WOMEN'S STUDIES

IN THIS CHAPTER a number of the contributors express the hunger many women feel: the hunger for a place to discuss, make connections, ask questions and apply knowledge; a place to realize what we already know, and to learn more. Academe is touted as such a place, but it fails and betrays many women. A myriad of oppressions including, but not limited to, racism, sexism, classism and ageism, intersect to define the differences in techniques used to ensure scholastic alienation and failure. In general, academe supports and sustains the silencing of women and contributes to feelings of "wrongness."

In First Impressions, a number of the contributors relay some of the conflicting feelings and unanswered questions that propelled them to enrol in a Women's Studies class for the first time. One woman writes about her uncertainty and fear of taking Women's Studies — her fear of releasing dormant knowledge: "I feel like I'm on the brink of knowing something; and having once understood, nothing will be quite the same." Another writes about her dissatisfaction and confusion with the inability and unwillingness of media, teachers and friends to answer her long list of queries.

A number of the contributors speak of the lack of understanding, the embarrassment, and even ridicule, they encountered when they spoke to their friends, families and, in one case, a stranger about Women's Studies. Attempts to dismiss, as trivial and pathological, Women's Studies and Women's Studies students add to their confusion and anger.

Holding Forth begins with a writer's deep sense of pleasure with her journal, her feelings of accomplishment inside a Women's Studies class and her wistful longing for inclusion. Throughout this section contributors discuss some of the effects of self-censorship and academic censorship, compare journal writing and scholastic writing and express the issues of safety inside Women's Studies.

This chapter communicates the sense of space, support and sheer relief many women feel inside Women's Studies. Not a safe, uncomplicated sense of relief but one that can be "'scary' ... [and] so good, so right, so home." It conveys the potential of Women's Studies to open doors to sites where all women's emotions, knowledges and different kinds of power can be acknowledged, challenged and sustained.

— *ELAINE*

First Impressions

Jackie Lynne

My anxiousness and fear of exposing myself.

I guess I've been afraid of taking Women's Studies. I've told myself that I could get by without this course of study. After all, there are other sociology credit options, aren't there?

The first day of class, looking around at the fresh faces, yet again, I'm more than aware of my age and the embarrassment (shame) of "late bloom." Someday, I'd like to write about my late arrival and what that's meant to me.

One reason I'm afraid of Women's Studies is because I feel like I'm on the brink of knowing something; and having once understood, nothing will be quite the same. During class last week I felt like crying a couple of times; during the readings I felt quite confused about a number of different points raised in the different articles. This is going to be a very disturbing course. I think I've known it would be and that's why I've avoided it.

It's hard just writing for me. I've never done it.

One question I'm still trying to answer from last week that's frustrating me is, "What's one thing that you've taught yourself?"

1. My mother taught me to knit, so that's out.
2. School taught me to read.
3. Writing is a gift. No one teaches you that.
4. How to survive a holocaust. My offender taught me that.
5. Singing is a gift.
6. So is dance.
7. So what the hell is "What's one thing I've taught myself?" It's a difficult one to answer because I see myself always in relation to someone else doing the teaching. My one consolation is my male partner in class also could not answer the question. I need more time, I think.

Varney Allis

Although it was hard to allow myself the time to write the journal entries, once I'd overcome the initial strangeness of it, I believe that it was the journal writing that transformed my life.

My first entry. I've been thinking of how and when to do this, and it's not happening as I expected. Instead of allowing myself to be in a tranquil setting, with plenty of time, I am sandwiching this into a free half-hour in my office, while I'm waiting for someone. I am afraid that if I don't at least begin now, I won't have anything written for tomorrow.

I decided to do this Women's Studies program on the recommendation of a friend whose kids go to the same school as mine. I seem to be at a crucial stage in my life (I hate the term "mid-life crisis" because it suggests a temporary aberration that one gets over before going back to the status quo). I need to make changes, and I think that gaining some insight into women's issues will help me to do this, or to understand why I am doing this. And, what am I doing anyway? I am trying to change the dynamics of my family, especially the relationship with my husband. I feel stuck, stalemated, stymied, stalled, screwed! Stomped on, stopped, stifled, suppressed — I didn't know these words were there — imagine if I chose other letters of the alphabet! Anyway, you probably get the idea.

Somewhere in all this — family politics? — is a dynamic that has been decidedly unfeminist, and that is what I want to get to the bottom of, and figure out how I can make it work, with or without the marriage. In case you are worried that I have too heavy an expectation of the course, I should add that I am seeing a therapist to work on this process. I see the course as a breath of fresh air into my life.

Laura Glomba

"It did not follow the rules. It was informal, personal, provocative, readable, jumbled, unapologetic, disorganized and inspiring."
—*HELEN LEVINE*

this is not going to be the safe, anonymous and predictable term i've come to expect.

all these words ...

"naming, personal, innervoice, women centred."

i have never looked at them the way we are being asked to do now.

there is this conflict going on. a feeling of being disturbed in some way.

connections being made, on all levels of thought. being "brought up"

looking, listening, wondering.

ugh.

why is this so bothersome? why do i feel i have been *let down* in some way — in my life?

why didn't i make the connections before?

"She must learn to speak/starting with I/starting with We/starting as the infant does/with her own true hunger/and pleasure/and rage."
— *MARGE PIERCY*

there is still the unsettling
settled
the stagnant
struggle
the apathy of harmony
the silenced
of the gentle and quiet.

Tanis Poole

My head is swimming with thoughts from the first Women's Studies class. I feel I have been immersed or am jumping off into something ... something so incredibly new for me.

The word "exploration" keeps coming to me with the realization of how little I know about Women's Studies. I know little, not only historically, politically, and philosophically, but perhaps most devastatingly, for me, is personally. I feel alienated or even virginal about a whole side of my personality/self and my relationship with myself (and accordingly with others) in what it means to me to be a woman. My initial reaction is to run, to not face what may be laborious and painful. But fortunately, the feelings of excitement and inspiration prevail and I look forward to the exploration ahead.

At the moment, the "swimming head" wants to predominate. I feel almost overwhelmed with the new ideas and possibilities taken in this afternoon. It feels like an unleashing or blossoming. Powerful feelings but a little out of control until I regain a focus — I don't have to do/learn/be everything at once. I have guides — my instructors and a structured course to help me in my exploration.

Pearl Kirby

This was my very first journal entry and I'm sorry to say I still don't have the answers to these questions because there is no answer to female oppression. You can't make sense out of something that is senseless. However, I have learned to deconstruct female oppression. Unfortunately I still get the old "Why are women protesting? We adore them and put them on pedestals. Why are they complaining?" It always ends with "women are so ungrateful!"

Some people don't seem to realize that women's "angelhood" is actually a prison. Any time a person is forced into a role (even the role of angel) it is not freedom. Besides, who benefits from this

role? Men or Women? If being on a pedestal is so great, why don't
men take it on? I'd be perfectly willing to sell my pedestal, it's only
twenty-nine years old; it's been continually used but it's virtually
indestructible.

I hardly know where to begin. There is so much I am feeling, but I don't know how to translate it into words. I have a lot of questions, that's one of the reasons I decided to take this course. I read newspapers and books. I watch movies and television. I talk to teachers and my friends, but no matter where I go I can't seem to find any answers, or if I do find an answer it doesn't make sense.

Sometimes I get really negative responses like: "Who cares? Why are you making such a big deal out of it? There isn't an answer, things just happen! It's a coincidence there's never been a female president. Besides women aren't interested in politics. Society is working just fine the way it is — why rock the boat? I don't know what women have to complain about, they get to stay home with their kids and watch soaps all day. I wish I could stay home all day and watch TV. Women have it good, we put them on pedestals, and they're still not satisfied...."

And on and on it goes. With responses like those, the more questions I ask the more confused I get.

I don't know if society will ever change or if the violence and oppression against women will ever stop. All I can do is to keep learning and asking questions.

Sometimes I get so discouraged I want to just pretend sexism doesn't exist. Sometimes it's almost easier to ignore it rather than fight it. I just don't understand why women are so oppressed. Why is there so much violence against women? Who made up these strange rules? Why do men make more money for the same job? Why aren't there birth control pills for men? How come Eve is so evil? Why didn't Adam share the blame?

I could fill up this whole book with my questions. Anyway, I'm glad I decided to take Women's Studies. I've only been in one class so far, but I'm enjoying it already. I know I'm going to learn a lot.

Tanis Poole

A door has opened....

For some time I have been interested in understanding how women-haters are created. These men have mothers, and many have sisters — there must be love shared among them. How are our roles as mothers and sisters involved in the socialization of these men? What is our possible influence to create change? How do I raise my son to be a critical thinker, a humanist, a feminist?

These questions were my starting point before yesterday's class on socialization and gender issues, but then my eyes were opened to something much closer to the bone — the socialization of women's relationships with women.

A seed was planted with my first Women's Studies class — it was new/different having women instructors (prior to coming to class I was filled with curiosity and mild trepidation by that fact). And to be among so many other women! Phew, "scary." But when I got to class, it felt so good, so right, so home. It was exciting to be there, all of us wanting to be there with the opportunity to learn/explore about ourselves as women.

The seed planted in that first class broke through — sprouted with yesterday's class. The poem "For Sharol Graves" [by Chrystos in *Not Vanishing*] is so beautiful — it really struck a chord/a space within me that I love — a sense of beauty, or peace that feels so special and separate from other areas of my life — a feeling I want to nourish. To hear that "our relationships with each other are taken from us by socialization," to realize that I have a wall to come down, to become aware of all the fear, distrust and guarded feelings that I bring to my relationships with women and thus myself — a door opened and I had to/have to examine myself.

The desire I have to work this issue out is not only for myself and other women but because I may be carrying a daughter — a thought that gives me a lot of mixed feelings. I want to feel better about women and myself as a woman, there are weeds to be taken out, I want to be clear for our relationship. I want the courage, peace and understanding to "raise my child not as a good girl or a bad girl but a girl who will grow to become a woman" (Jennifer Martin, *Tales from a Broken Heart*).

Debbra Brown

At the time I was fresh to college — excited and overwhelmed by information and access — finding my voice. But frustrated by attitude/arrogance/oblivion of those I'd felt were my friends

PIGGY'S GOT THE BLUES

Whirring
      round the house
I go
      laundry
run to
      the store
           find a book
need a quarter
      throw it in the dryer
okay
      done done
What
      to do
papers
      piled
           each their own world
strewn
      round my world
door
      knocks   friends stop
thanks too busy
      phone
           rings
ear
      meets whining

short patience gone
        want?
whining
        more
bus   soon
        must go! where?
Women's Studies
        question waits
halting awkwardly
        carefully
I explain ... perspectives roles
        equality   or
                                    lack of
Oh
        is there a man's studies class?
rage
        within
                burns and boils
threatens
                to let me scream all the
way to class
        curtly
                I reply why offer a class
that rules our lives   society
        in all our classes
bristle
        reply comes
really there is no inequality
        I think things aren't that bad
talks more
        clarifying the truth
so even
        I can understand
one
        final whine
take care
        I mumble
as
        I choke
                back a scream.

B. J.

I'm still trying to sort out the reality of my family versus what I want to believe. I can acknowledge all the positive aspects. I need to also acknowledge some of the things I find hard to accept.

As I sit down at my computer, I am so grateful for my space. It has been an eventful week, travelling to Ontario for my grandfather's funeral. During the seven-hour journey, I read various articles for my Women's Studies course. My grandfather had spent many happy years teaching at a university and excelling in the academic world so I figured he would be pleased to know I was making good use of the time to "study."

The content of the course is intensely interesting to me and when I read, I feel like a sponge. I feel very much in conflict at the moment, having spent a week in the company of my white, upper-middle-class, highly educated, and quite traditional, extended family. Many people questioned me, "So what are you up to these days?" and I answered with enthusiasm about going back to school (part-time) for the first time in about ten years. I saw the veiled look in their eyes after they discovered I am taking a Women's Studies course. Some enthusiasm was expressed by some of the women. The minister who looked after the funeral service was very interested. He acknowledged the fact that God has been traditionally viewed in our society as male and as he spoke to me, he switched quite freely from "he" to "she" as he talked about the God of his understanding. He told me his daughter was raped at the age of eleven by a male teacher staying in their home as a guest. There was a very painful silence between us for a few moments.... My mother was upset because the minister referred to God once as a "she" during the funeral service. She felt it very inappropriate for my grandfather. This makes me feel very sad. I also feel a tremendous desire to take my mother's hurt away.

My grandmother is almost ninety and is a very sad woman too this time. She too was a professor at a university for many years and during her lifetime was married to two very successful men. A number of times throughout my visit, she mentioned how upset she was at radical feminists. She told me about the kind and loving men in her life, including various family members and many work associates. I didn't know what to say to her and had no desire to "defend" my position as a feminist. I am puzzled by this defence of men. By stating that I am taking a Women's Studies course it seemed to me that it meant to her that I hate men. I too am surrounded by men I love and am saddened by her reaction.

My mother apologized as she introduced me to her high-school friends as a feminist. "I don't mean anything negative by that," she explained to them. She wants to be proud of her daughter going back to school (this is a very academic family) and is uncomfortable with it. I have said very little and tried to just observe. I am comforted by the fact that my eighteen-year-old female cousin and I were asked to be pallbearers along with four male family members, and the majority of the women in my family have excelled and continue to excel in many professions.

At times, I feel like a subversive, radical person (me!) in their eyes and fight an overwhelming desire to fit in and be "part of." I see myself as a white, middle-class heterosexual, quite traditional woman (living slightly above the poverty line at present). I am trying to understand and name the reasons behind my rage and periodic feelings of low self-worth and self-hatred, trying to put it in a context I can make sense of. I want to understand and hopefully start to change my sexist, racist, homophobic and classist ways of being. I also want to belong and be loved and understood. I am amazed at the reaction I received from my family by merely stating I was taking a Women's Studies course and feel somewhat despairing about it. It will be very helpful to be back in a supportive environment this week.

Jane Swann

"You're taking WOMEN'S STUDIES???
What for ... are you GAY OR SOMETHING?
Who wants to study women ...
they never did anything did they?"

I am standing in the registration line-up,
The woman behind the obnoxious man says
"That course CHANGED MY LIFE!"

Sounds like a cheap ad for losing weight
Sounds like some scary religious flip
But I'm not changing my mind....
I am pulled, unaware by what, to the counter....

Registered and in class
I'm nervous....

ALL THE WOMEN LOOK SO BEAUTIFUL ...
What on earth am I doing here????
"The most ugly, disgusting, unintelligent..." I mean above
everyone else, "beautiful, intelligent, perfect..." I mean ...

The course proceeds....

"HOLY FUCKING SHIT" we say after the class

We exhaust every swear word we know....
NO ... NO we say
YES ... YES ...YESSSSSS we say....

Women's Studies was my first comprehensive introduction to feminism. I left the class one million miles from where I started ... and
somehow ended up much closer to myself than I had been in years.
The class was hard ... at moments it was sheer pain. At twenty years

old I began the process of realizing the widespread existence of misogyny. It hurt. I remembered all of the times in my life when I had been hurt by men. I realized that the people I valued most in my life ... my brother, my boyfriends, my father, my teachers, my priests, had something in common ... they had all hurt me and were men. The information in the class ripped my years of denial surrounding my sexual abuse apart.... I can't describe the state of mind I had that term.... I can't describe what I learned ... it just won't fit into these words....

I mostly learned
to trust women, to like women, to not be afraid of women
and to love women actively

I also learned
not to give away my soul to men, to say goodbye to the
men who were hurting me, and to separate the concept of
"power over me" from "love" (a whole load of poetic guitar
players with regular erections and little brain capacity hit
the road with haste).

I learned to dream....
What if there were no men in the world ... no war ... no
guns ... no rape ...? Imagine ... women loving each other ...
in every way possible....

I learned reality
Even if the men were gone ... their world would exist in
our heads ... it would take so much work to unlearn their
ways of domination....

I learned that one half of my "self-esteem" was on the bottom of the ocean and the other half was soaring above the sun.

Finally, I met the MOST AMAZING WOMEN. For the first time in my life I actually was stretched to the limits of AWE over women ... the wisdom which these women left each other will last forever....

"THAT COURSE CHANGED MY LIFE!!!!"
I was standing behind a rather nervous-looking woman in the long-line up for registration.... She looked back at me with a frightened look ... but she kept going up to the counter....

HOLDING FORTH

I DON'T REMEMBER KEEPING a diary when I was younger, but the image of those small plastic-covered books with the tiny lock and keys remains strong. Just the mention of them elicited a round of knowing laughter among the contributors in our discussions (see Chapter Five). Diaries like those were crucial for many women who felt very alone growing up, with no one to talk to who would understand.

The classroom journal has some of the same qualities of self-reflection and self-healing as the diary. Writing to an instructor at the same time as thirty other women and men are writing can also be quite a new experience. Very often, women have noted that the response to their journals, from instructors and other classmates, helped them realize that they were not crazy or alone — that there are other women who have similar thoughts, questions, ideas and uncertainties.

In this section, contributors write of the value of their journals in mapping their own learning, noting the ground from which they speak and their passage through and beyond it. Sometimes that ground can be a little shaky, and these entries also reflect a range of problems that women encounter in writing. Many of these conflicts revolve around dealing with the voices in their heads — the unnamed but ubiquitous internal editor, the harsh voice of judgement of past teachers, or of "the politically correct." Two entries discuss daring to speak out loud, when their own internal voice is making them "sick to death," and whether it's "nice" or not to do so. Despite these obstacles, women are holding forth.

— *DOROTHY*

Gina Marina Cifuentes Faena

Quiet now, so quiet as I sit here in my living room on my old beat-up, found in a garage, 1970s, plaid, sectional, square sofa, sponge wrapped in big-print, colour material to make cushions. The house now quiet ... kids in bed dreaming, shallow breathing, quiet, soft faces, soft small round arms and legs resting after playing hard. Quiet that makes time stand still. I close my eyes to hear the quiet, only hear the cracks of the walls, so quiet, occasional brushes of chimes that touch each other like touches of persons just starting to fall in love, those brushes of passion that you think the other person doesn't notice but you know they do and they know you do. Brushes so soft just barely, just enough, the refrigerator turns on humming along, quiet returns when it's tired and rests.

I love this journal. Every wednesday when it will be returned I hug and caress it. I wish I could dive in deeper into these words like diving in a hidden swimming hole in the forest, cold, mysterious, water rushing all over my body touching every pore every little hair, these small entries I feel they could, they do take me deep. They make me remember. I stay under long and take a breath when my lungs and cheeks burst. I come up out of the cold, refreshing, tingling water and laugh, shake, burst. I love the feeling. Like when you sort of jump out of the water and breathe in hard, to warm your body and then sink slink like a smooth otter again deep in the water. Hard pebbles under your feet, it's easier to swim all the way to the shoreline and walk to the towel.

There was quiet very similar to this quiet tonight during our presentation. Long quiet, very, very quiet. It's not that often I hear that type of quiet. Yeah there was the slide projector, the voices, the clicks of the slides moving, but there was this extra quiet. I heard it, it was very loud like cymbals in a band, like playground noises, how can that be? Cymbals crashing — why does the quiet seem to use cymbals? I remember everything, every slide, all our words. I wish I could have transported myself to be there as the audience, to hear the words as new words, the slides as new slides, the candles, our voices. It worked, yes it worked, all those faces when the lights turned on, they were frozen, no reaction, no, too much reaction so there was no reaction. I didn't want to leave tonight to face my hard metal car, hard straight streets, other world. I wanted to stay in that warm halcyon room. It was like the last page is running out of words but you want to read more so you go back through the book and find passages just to taste the flavour again, like a dish of food, you want the taste to linger, I lingered, the candles, the leaves, the smell like the smell of someone you love, you know their smell you smell closer when you are with them, you can taste the smell.

I write, I am writing again not now I mean, I mean my words are getting put down on paper. Words, if spoken to many would be misunderstood words. My journal, my listener. My journal it understands me, well of course it does, it is me. Well I mean I need to speak all these thoughts I speak out loud but I feel like no one listens but this journal does, always more room, but I need people too, people who understand me, really me, I guess I need some different kinds of friends not just regular day-to-day friends but creative? is creative the right word. well, maybe friends with depth? exploring friends maybe? Explorers? know-where-I'm-coming-from friends, not judgemental friends. I love people. Actually I made four new friends, including me. I knew me a long time ago but she took a trip and now she's back. Good to be home. Must write about my trip. I will. It's late, with this quiet I go to bed.

Bad Girl Liar

Academia demands an objective voice. Finding and using that voice continues to challenge me.

Don't edit. I can't not edit. I've just spent two days of my life editing. Trying to fix what I want to say. I am going crazy trying to fit my life into this academic structure and here I am allowed not to fit .... I'm confused. I am angry. This makes no sense. I should be glad that here I can blurt, but my "clean it up ... neaten it up" response is so automatic that I can't just let it go.

They're trying to make me crazy. Who? Who are they? Why don't you name them? You can't, that's why. It's all in your head. You're just trying to blame your inadequacies on external things. You don't make any sense. When you do make sense it comes out to nothing. Can't you do anything right? Can't you talk about course content? No, because immediately then I edit. Do you want to know the truth? I am surprised to read about women whom I know of in the folk music scene. Surprised that they are the pioneers and sad — because I write songs that have a message to sing to the world and I'm tired of breaking ground. I want to be just one of the girls .... I want to belong to a rich heritage, not be one who stands alone. One of a few. I can't get past how hopeless it looks. I just want to quit. So there.

Michelle Elizabeth Neilson

I'm still slightly phobic about writing. But the more I let myself write, the more I understand its power as a tool for getting in touch with my true self and sharing that self with others.

Well, here it is November and I am plagued by several papers in my different classes. I have an extreme writing phobia that started in high school. I don't know how I did it but I managed to graduate from high school without writing a single essay, research paper or book report. I think I am so afraid of writing crap or not backing myself up with enough facts etc. I was so paralysed before that I used to just not hand them in. In my first year at Langara I put off doing my English research paper so long that I just didn't do it, it was worth 30 percent (miraculously I still passed) I have managed over the last past couple of semesters to actually produce my papers, but I basically threw them together, I really haven't given them much thought and often haven't even read the books. I really don't think I'm just lazy, I think it's more of a fear of success and a fear of failure. It's like I'm paralysed.

I think now I also feel stifled by the expected writing styles of most classes. This stems partly from a comment that a female professor made to me about my paper in first year. She said, "You write like a woman." She went on to explain that if I ever wanted to get anywhere in the "academic world" I would have to learn to write more objectively. She said that I wrote the way I talked and that it was no good. She had been told the same thing in her early years of university and had eventually learned to write properly. So I guess even when I can write personally, i.e., in Women's Studies and Religious Studies, I am still afraid. I feel like my knowledge has to be forced out of me by an essay in a final exam or test. That appears to be the only time I will rise to the challenge.

Bad Girl Liar

Denial is a powerful way of protecting the self from being overwhelmed, but it doesn't necessarily foster growth.

My writing does make the ground below my feet more solid — but mainly when I am engaged in the actual writing. Sometimes (often) I reread my thoughts and then mock myself for such grandiose ideas. As if simply stating something could make it real. Although I realize that this self-mockery is part of a long-standing habit — it seems in some ways prudent. For if I run too far, too fast, I may discover myself — like a cartoon character over the edge of a cliff with only air beneath my feet.

Ideas of healing and balance, then, do not reflect the actual events. This inner struggle — to recognize the steps that need to be made, while at the same time acknowledging my paltry progress — is perpetual. You see my paradox! If I do not acknowledge the courageous step I have/am taking, then the self-doubt will rise up and swallow my perspective. If I allow the courage to sustain me, then I risk overestimating my strength and progress — thus becoming vulnerable to danger. One battle won does not guarantee victory, yet

surely succeeding in battle — even one time — counts for something. I am greatly blessed in that I have clear perceptions of the
walls that rise around my progress. I remember not to underestimate
them. I try to acknowledge their initial purpose and thereby avoid
throwing out the baby with the bathwater.

Small steps, successive approximations, consistent effort — I
will by this method reach my goals. Dream the big dream, then
identify the small steps along the path to it.

Karen Egger

*This was an important piece of thinking/writing for me, one that
has served me well since.*

Reflected some, after talking with you briefly after class Tuesday
night, that I didn't really feel particularly safe in the class, just more
comfortable than I did last term, primarily because I knew more
people.

I think that you are doing a really great job of facilitating a safe
environment. My lack of security comes from a doubt in my ability
to deal with others' reactions/judgements about what I say or don't
say. I censor myself — what I will/won't say — according to what
others may think. I would like to be able to put out what I'm thinking, even if I'm not sure it's "politically correct," or that others may
disagree, or think I'm _____. Which, on a rational, theoretical
level shouldn't matter, but it's in my body, this fear of other's reac-
tion/judgement. It's a major obstacle for me to overcome. If I have
something to say that I'm unsure of in terms of its reception, I'd like
to speak out more.

So that is what safety is for me, a group that would receive what
I say ... me, with respect of difference, curiosity, non-judgement.
And such a group may exist but I find this class to feel somewhat
unsafe. I have realized in the writing that I can create my own safety
as well as fulfilling my desire to speak out, by speaking out only if

I'm prepared to deal with judgement, disapproval, etc. I need to feel strong within myself to do that, and so sometimes will, sometimes not, depending on what I feel my ability is to handle others' responses. I also recognize that you have in the past intervened in such situations and I'm sure would do so again if necessary.

This topic area feels scary though, like peeling away the layers to some very vulnerable, child-like, uncertain, fragile place.

Jennifer Conroy

This is me as a young poet struggling to believe in the value of my words and importance of my voice. In retrospect, I can say that the struggle has paid off.

Do you know how much i have written over the years? I have journals, calendars, note-margins, filled with what i've been thinking and saying on the inside of my head. When i can't sleep i write in my journal until my arm aches or i'm so tired that my words are no longer coherent. But what have I said? Next to nothing. I've gotten sick to *death* of the voice inside my head. And maybe that's because i wasn't saying things out loud to people. It seems so simple, but i think that i have to put my hands on my shoulders and lean in real close and whisper in my own ear, "What will happen if you say it? What is the worst thing?" What to say, when to say it, to whom, how, and when to keep my silence as strength?

Laura Glomba

between solid lines.
hmmm.
i am hungry, ravenous, devouring.
i am filled with anger.
      filling up with anger.
      disgusting anger.
i am sad too.

---

i listened to her — at first inarticulate
                     she broke down for a
                     moment
                     gained composure
                     burst forth with such
                     passionate articulation
                     and powerful too
ANGER.
i heard courage. taking a chance by speaking.
ruffle SOME feathers?
so, fucking, what! why do we always have to be so nice.

Chapter Two

NAMING

Chapter Two

NAMING

THE FRENCH AND LATIN roots of the word "journal" both mean "daily," and it is the subject of the everyday that women most often write about in their journals. When women's words and experience have for so long been actively silenced, writing about the everyday can have revolutionary significance. In this section, the contributors name some of the everyday forces that have shaped their experience and their knowing. They describe a reality that is worlds apart from what we usually see on television, or can read about elsewhere. Most of the entries are descriptive; many contributors also frame them within an examination and critique of their place in the larger society.

In my reading of these entries, I was struck by two constants. The first was that, despite its rapidly changing definition and role, "family" remains very important for most women. Read as a whole, this section paints a description of a social grouping with many different variations in the identities of blood and adopted mothers, fathers and children, and in the roles of mixed, blended and extended families.

Over and over again, the contributors describe how they are creating new forms of family among the rifts of the old. Individually their stories tell of working through the grief of separation from birth families, communities and cultures. As a set they begin to fill in the biographies of women who have been affected by interrelated governmental policies and regulations in such areas as adoption, the treatment of First Nations citizens and the treatment of immigrants. The thread running through many of these accounts is redress, remembering the past in order to create new kinds of supportive relations in the present.

The everyday role of violence in women's lives was the other constant. It is not only the subject matter of the last section, but permeates the two preceding sections in this chapter — Body and Imaging and Sexuality. The violence is there in the physical harm done to women's bodies and the emotional damage to their psyches. The contributors not only name their own experience of this violence, but also begin to unmask the identities of some of the individuals, and especially of the larger social forces, that perpetrate it. In doing this, they also recount their own daily resistance to the violence — a daily resistance that includes reclaiming the connection between body, identity, sexuality and relationship.

— *DOROTHY*

WHO AND WHAT IS "FAMILY"?

I SWIM A LOT. As I go back and forth doing laps, I sort through some of the bigger questions in my life. One evening before Women's Studies class, the student journal entries for that week, my own family dilemmas, and the class content I had prepared were all rolling around together as my hands slapped the water. After completing my laps I sat on the edge of the pool contemplating the three dressing room signs. One was for women, one for men and the third for families. I wondered if sitting there long enough observing who decided to use the family dressing room would help me come to any conclusions. Unfortunately, no one exited and I was left contemplating the "family" sign with its familiar stick drawings of one adult figure in a skirt, one in pants and two child figures in the same prescribed female and male apparel. The clarity that I carried with me from this event was that the section of the course on the politics of the family was vital. The different contradictions each of us finds between our realities and the prevailing ideologies and social policies would provide the compass for the class discussions.

The journal writing during the course constantly reminds me of our variety of experiences, needs and visions for change, both inside and outside our own families. It also challenges me to include students' issues as we analyze the larger forces that have an impact on families. As you read this part of the book, I think you will see how hard it would be to read these journals and not have them profoundly affect the breadth of the course content. The writing provides the heartbeat for the class, making sure many voices are represented and connecting theories to experiences.

And, each year, the journal writings carve out new definitions of family, motherhood, and relationships.

— *PATTY*

As one of the contributors to this section, I realized that, for me and many women, trying to figure out our families is an integral part of the process of understanding ourselves. Situating ourselves within our families — learning who and where we come from, what family histories have been hidden or lost, what and how politics had an impact on our families' lives; how each of our families cope, helps us in explaining ourselves to ourselves and in locating ourselves in the world. The contributors to this section come from many different backgrounds and experiences, yet, whatever feelings each of our families evoke (pain, joy, sorrow, anger, love, loneliness ...) family — our own definitions of family — are central.

As I read this section, what became clear is that the reality of family is not as we have been told: constrained by, and sometimes opposed to it, few of our families really fit the Western, father-headed, nuclear model. Each contributor describes her own version of family as she knows them. Many of the entries reflect the ongoing struggles to recognize and understand the impact of the myriad interconnections between social, political and personal issues. These broad dimensions of family life and struggle remind me that I am just beginning to explore the range of Who and What Is "Family".

— *ELAINE*

Julie Elise Archer

This is one of the family stories I did not hear when I was growing up. While I wish I had, now that I do know about them I think about my Aunties Beezie and Evelyn a lot and wonder about their life together.

My grandfather arrived from Ireland yesterday. He is going to stay with my parents for a month. He is eighty-six and very healthy, which is why it was so strange to see him so exhausted from his flight, so distant in his weariness, so elderly, as Mum said. In the car on the way to Mum and Dad's, Grandpa and Mum were talking about the time Auntie Beezie lived with them when Mum was small. I had forgotten about that. Grandpa said it was when Evelyn Riley died.

Evelyn Riley?

I asked Grandpa about Evelyn Riley. When Vera (Auntie Beezie) was in her twenties, she worked for her father, my great-grandfather, who was a solicitor. When he became ill and retired, she lived with him and looked after him. At that time she met a woman called Evelyn Riley. Evelyn lived with relatives nearby, and she and Beezie "struck up an amazing friendship" (Grandpa's words).

When my great-grandfather died, they moved in together, and Beezie got a job at the Dublin heraldry office. Evelyn also worked in the city, so the two of them went in to work together and came home together. Then Evelyn got a transfer to London, so Beezie quit her job and they moved to London, where Beezie worked as an administrator at St. Thomas' Hospital.

Beezie and Evelyn spent their summer holidays in County Kerry with my mum's family. They grew to love Kerry, and when they retired they bought Curraduff, the house I remember from my childhood holidays. They hadn't lived there too many years when Evelyn got sick and died. My granny, Beezie's sister, went to stay with Beezie in Curraduff, and then Beezie came back with Granny to live with Mum's family in Limerick. Grandpa advised her not to sell Curraduff, although she wanted to, because he thought she might not like Limerick, and she didn't. Before too long she moved back to Curraduff, where she lived for the rest of her life.

I remember Beezie as the great-aunt who wore trousers and glasses and had a nasal voice. I remember choosing a tiny ship in a bottle when she invited my sister and me to take something from her glass cabinet home with us. I never met Evelyn and I don't remember hearing about her as I grew up, which I am sorry about. Who knows, I might have come out as a lesbian untroubled when I was a child rather than guilty when I was twenty-one, knowing that my great-aunts Beezie and Evelyn had come before me, strong and loving. But I'm glad I know about them now.

Leslie Rene Lo

Upon reflection, my mother's passing seemed a necessary provoca-
tion to overcome the unacknowledged barriers we both shared.
Were it not for her unconventional perseverance I would not have
developed the tools needed to recognize the ever-present subtleties
left to me in her legacy.

I've included this journal entry for it emphasizes my own personal
need to understand my relationship with my mother. When I think
about mothers and daughters I go back to the days of my grandmother's (po-po) time. I recall my mom telling me stories about
gong-gong (grandfather). He was quoted time over for his unwillingness to support baby girls. "Why have girls? They cost too much
money. Chickens would be better; at least they produce an income.
Girls just end up marrying and leaving to support another family."
Mom would tell me how hard po-po had to fight, how she had to
negotiate the trade of life-long subservience and silence for the life
of her two baby girls. Po-po had zero access to her rights as a
Chinese Canadian woman. There were no rights anyway. She was
stuck in a typical race/class/status void that all the other Chinese
immigrant women were. Her only escape was death. She achieved
this mercifully at the age of forty-two.

My own mother — po-po's daughter — had lived, day in and
day out, with the guilt of her mother's passing, thinking that maybe
if she was a boy then the hardship would have been lessened. Both
po-po and her daughter had no way of identifying the politics of
their predicament. Gender- race- and class-oriented barriers were
planted into every aspect of their lives. They did not have access to
the women's movement of the 1960s, they did not know words and
concepts like "empowerment," "voice," "take back the power," "naming," "oppression," "social change." What they knew was survival.

At seventeen, my mother was barely out of high school when
she found herself engaged to be married to a man twenty years her
senior. Gong-gong had arranged for his best friend to wed his bur-
densome daughter. She spent seven years cooking, cleaning, and
bearing his children, choking on her silence. One day she conjured

up the courage to leave. She escaped, but not without battle wounds. He would not let her have the children. Her choices were few. Go back and suffer a life like her mother's, or fight him and try to win the kids back. She never saw those kids again. The courts were not about to award three young children to an unemployed, uneducated Chinese woman who didn't even have a place to live. Like po-po, my mother was up against institutionalized barriers. Her last resort was nursing school. A convent took her in, and trained her to work with the poor.

When I was born, my real dad stuck around until I was two. The following seventeen years of my mother's life were filled with a combination of joy, desperation and silence. I was to be her voice, her knowledge and her refuge. She raised me as best as any single, working Asian mother could. Her strength and perseverance showed us through the tough times. All she ever wanted in life was for me to have the power to fight the system. Our relationship was based on the basics — survival, need and unconditional love. She was very reserved about teaching me to be Chinese. The less I knew about it the better chance I had of fighting the racism and discrimination to come in later years. As a result I was raised very anglo. I learned the ways of the *Lo-Fun* (White Devil) and in essence was equipped to fight fire with fire.

As a mother she faced many opposing forces. She had no way of knowing that her internal struggle was shared by thousands of women just like her. She didn't know that she was allowed to join forces with these women to promote social/political change. She didn't know if she was raising her daughter properly. She thought white women went to school to learn such things.

As a daughter I now find myself filled with sorrow and regret. I can never thank her for her support. I can never tell her that she was just as smart as the rest of them. When she died, I was too young to put our realities into perspective. I had not yet found our voice. Inside of me rests my mother's will. She held open the doors for me, but would only stand at their thresholds, urging me to go forward in her most reassuring voice. Her sacrifices were totally selfless. She died when I was nineteen — just as I was coming back to get her to take her through those doors with me. To show her that she did the right thing.

Now her spirit lives vicariously through me. All of my power and strength goes towards discovery. For my mother I will identify her oppressors, and bring them down. She can rest peacefully knowing that her grand daughters will continue her fight.

Kasthuri Moodley-Ismail

Sacrifices, challenges and pain present themselves in many ways. For me, they have been the main ingredients of my progress and inevitable success in everything I do. The combined strength of my family is attributable to my strength and courage to move on.

Alone ... among twenty-seven million people?

Even though it sounds impossible, it is true for me; I do sometimes feel alone among Canada's twenty-seven million people. It makes me think back to a sunny day almost ten years ago....

The day I left South Africa was a day of mixed emotions. I was leaving to find and experience freedom for myself and my family. I came to terms with the fact that I may not see my family for decades. Well, it has been a decade since.

I've grown up, matured and become my "own woman," and nobody but me has noticed and appreciated these changes. There is no joy that I can get from my personal accomplishments if I can't share it with my family — a family full of caring and support. What price have I paid for freedom of movement and speech, human rights and education?

Recently I've been taking "stock" of my struggles and accomplishments, and after some brainstorming I've decided to go back home. Not now, not tomorrow, but one day. I will share the same lifestyle, laugh at the same jokes and travel the same road. Then we will have to come back to Canada, and again the day will come and the mixed emotions will arise, the airplane will be looming over me and the flight attendant will be ushering me to my seat.... Why do I sound depressed, I ask? Is it because I just got my period last night? Oh damn!

Gina Marina Cifuentes Faena

I read Milagros Paredes' article in the reading package. Spanish
Filipina article, Me not spanish filipina but same mixed feelings.
Not whole, denial of self, mixed person me. It would be so much
easier to be full race person. Not so much struggle. But I'm not ego-
centric either, so that's a plus. But I feel like pieces are missing, my
grandmother on my mother's side was maya, but relatives in
Guatemala deny. Same as Spanish shit going on in "From the Inside
Out." "Oh no your abuela wasn't maya she was _____." No word,
they didn't have a word. "But your NONO Abuelo from Italy, he was
Blah Blah Blah...." My nono went to Guatemala to get away from
his blood in Italy. He married maya, he loved that maya. He didn't
give a shit about his blood line in Italy he gave up all that b.s. property etc. He wanted a real life.

I didn't know my abuelo, but in the summer I went to his grave
and abuela's grave with the kids. We found the grave, brought flowers, touched the wall in the basement of the grave. A small mau-
soleum, a small building he is in the basement with abuela. The kids
and i went down the wooden ladder, left the flowers, sat outside. We
were silent. Abuela and Abuelo were there, they came out to see us.
We felt them hug us. We were not able to leave. They touched our
faces, smiled, floated around us, told us they loved us, their grand-
child, their great-grandchildren de Canada. We smiled and cried.

I wanted to talk to them — Know me, See me — hold their
hands, hear their voices, smell them. We stayed long, we cried lots.
They didn't want us to leave. We had to. I wanted to know why they
named my mother Liberty America, why she is artistic, why she
wanted something different. All her sisters have typical italian and
spanish names. They just floated around us. We sat still, we hugged
each other. One day I will go back and make a proper tombstone.
They have no tombstone. I will bring them one.

Laura Mervyn

Four years later my grandmother died. Her legacy to me was her strength and humour, and my realization that she lived a profoundly feminist life in her actions, though she would never have named herself so. Ruth Mervyn, I thank you for your model of how to be a strong woman in a world not made for us.

Last night I phoned my grandmother in Honolulu. Since I last spoke to her she has gone from her own small apartment to a "convalescent home." Her apartment had a banana tree in the backyard and just enough clean, immaculate space. Grandma said she'd die in six weeks if they put her in a nursing home — and there she is.

Last January, when she had a heart attack, my sister and I flew down to help. The week we were there became one of my most precious experiences. When we brought her home from the hospital, she was confused and very weak. She thought that she was expected to look after us — after all, she always had! Her confusion cleared up fast once she got into her own home, and her sense of humour soared. She wasn't able, at first, to even feed herself. We had to take her (all 170 pounds of her) to the bathroom, set her on the toilet, wipe her off, etc. I have never felt so close to anyone. Some of our most precious moments were sitting in the tiny bathroom (all three of us), waiting for her to finish having a bowel movement and being awed by the dignity and humour with which she carried it off. She has such a strong sense of who she is that she didn't lose anything to shame or embarrassment. I want to live a long time. I'll have to, to ever equal her. I love her so much.

I phoned her last in the nursing home and we talked politely to each other. I was so filled with love and pain and anger, I couldn't reach across and bridge that gap. It's not fair that although she worked all her life, she hasn't got the money to control her own destiny by hiring a companion, a nurse etc. Tonite, I'm calling her again, and if it doesn't work out I'll call again.

Debbra Brown

Indian half breed
             dirty
      I see her head hanging in shame
             pain buried by years
she skirts
             dances around my questions
since a child
             fierce pride and oneness
with those around
             things of nature
Oh
             that was your Mother's side, not
US dear
             you got confused
yet
             tall and dark you stand before me
your lies
             scream past me
frustration
                    builds mounts within
world
      so close   so far
how can I be one but neither?
      once again
                    my "culture" questioned
Yes, I have native ancestors
      still I am not, no I did not
live on a reserve
                    it is not shame that quiets me
how can I claim something
             for which I have not yet paid the price.

Iris Fabiola Naguib

I AM

My heritage?
both white and Brown
some say half-breed
I say proud
proud to be a part of both

No one else's shame
has to be mine
If you have a problem
with where I place myself
read between my lines

Yes
I am biracial
Yes
I am woman
But first
I am spirit
I am soul
I AM

Pat J.

As I read some of the stories in the Women's Studies reading package, each of them sparked a memory. I remember from a very young age that I had this feeling and I didn't know what it was. Today I know it's fear. All of this fear came from the DIA [Department of Indian Affairs] who were putting a lot of pressure on my folks. This pressure was to have us children go to residential school. My parents had to make choices. They knew that if and when we went we would never be home again for a very long time. During that era, I think the early 1950s, priests, nuns, etc. had authority to let you visit home, or not at all. Most of the time it was not at all.

There were many other things that were important to me at that time, although I didn't know it then. My grandmother has been coming up in my mind recently. She has been the most important person in my life. She was like my second mother. Before residential school, half of my time was spent with her. So it was my grandmother who taught me values, culture and language.

So when my parents had to make choices about us kids, there were major consequences. They knew we would lose all of the things that meant something to us — culture, language and values. All of this happened many years ago. For the past seven years I have been on a search. There were many issues I had to face, and some of them very painful. Some of the culture was completely lost, but at least today I know who I am. And I can name feelings and be honest and feel good about being a First Nations citizen.

Jackie Lynne

Written because I needed to be reminded I am a writer. I had not written for twenty years.

[These next three entries were written throughout the term.]

A REASON FOR MAYWOODS

Her young body shifts in its torn position on the bed. The tightness of her stitches between the hospital sheets reminds her of why she is here. She must get up! Her ragdoll limbs disjointedly obey an ancient and primal command. She is not aware of her senses leaving, of how flat and muted the arrival of this moment is. A faceless clock has disappeared into a silent wall. Someone has stolen the colours from her room. She doesn't mind. Slowly, she rises to a bedside flower she does not smell. She looks down at her feet, which point to a floor she knows she will not feel.

Standing now, she stares into the greyness of the corridor. As she nears the ward door, seemingly from out of nowhere appears the brigadier. At 10:00 a.m. precisely, every morning, her aged, quavering voice can be heard singing hymns everywhere throughout the hospital except in the washrooms. The girl takes her baths at that time.

She's looking at the brigadier's mouth. It has become a black and gaping hole. Above this hole are two smaller ones. Her nose is missing. The brigadier is now two-dimensional, a cut-out figure. The girl recalls another time and smiles to herself. Turning in the direction of garbled sounds, she sees the singular, gaping hole opening and closing mechanically. This old woman is barren, and the girl knows that cut-outs do not give birth. She wants to scream into the holes, but it would be pointless because the brigadier casts no shadow.

Leaving behind the gaping holes, she starts down the corridor. She remembers a scene from a television show — or perhaps she's just imagining it. A den mother's cub has gone missing. The mother is frantic in her search. The girl cannot look into the animal's eyes; she's afraid she might recognize something. Its anguished cries relentlessly echo in her ears. The corridor seems endless.

All professionals involved with her delivery encourage her to embrace the experience. So, she watched her baby's entrance into the world, felt her womb being emptied. Every four hours, her daughter comes to her for feeding. She wants to give suck, but has been advised this would not be good for the baby. Today, the girl fed her child for the last time. Her bound and swollen breasts are weeping.

In a little while, both mother and child will leave this hospital, but not together. Upon her return home, she will be taught to pretend this never happened. She is a desperate student.

The end of the corridor is very near. It is here that the nursery can be found. She knows. Many, many times, she has come to stand before the separating glass. Now it's receding in her careful quickened pace. She reaches the door and hears the starched voice of a ward nurse. For one knowing moment, their eyes meet and hold. The young girl is told that mothers are not allowed in the nursery.

SEPT. 22 '92

Circles of completion ... relationships and the reciprocity of need.

Twenty-three years ago and a stone's throw away from where I'm sitting presently, I was giving birth to a baby girl. From the moment of relinquishment, I gave up, also, the name "mother." At least, I thought I had. Today has been such a reflective day. I can recall so many details. I watched her birth. Even before she was completely outside of me, her mouth was open and she was hollering. Alert, is how the doctors described her.

I've said a mental "Happy Birthday" to her many times today. She's on the other side of the world, intent on having the world be her oyster.

This weekend I will meet with her adopted mom for the first time. I wonder what will happen. I'm scared, excited, and a little bit envious of this woman. I feel like I really need this "meeting of mothers" someplace inside where I still can't cry. Her name is Rose. She sounds so frail on the phone. She's been a good parent and provided a safe and loving home for my child. But, still, I guess, in spite of knowing how well my child was raised and how much gratitude I have towards her adoptive family, I still wish in my heart of hearts that I had kept her.

UNWRAPPED GIFTS

The title says it all.

Over Christmas I met with my daughter's adoptive mom and dad for the second time. At one point, I was seated between both her parents, ankle-deep in family photos. I knew I was in the midst of something very, very magical.

The husband went into the kitchen, leaving his wife and me alone in the livingroom. I was hanging tinsel on their tree — my favourite Christmas thing to do. In a very soft voice (so her husband wouldn't hear), my daughter's mom told me that she had given up a daughter when she was eighteen years old and that she's never told anyone — not her husband or her children. (shame) The daughter she gave up would be my age.

I can't begin to describe what this whole experience has meant for me. I watched the movie of Margaret Laurence's *The Diviners* and thought about human relationships coming full circle, how we come together to heal, to resolve conflicts.

I have been very blessed by how this Christmas went and hope to one day write a short story about it — without sounding too sentimental.

Christie Woodin

My brother and sister-in-law had their first baby last weekend — a girl. The whole family is ecstatic, and that's all anyone talks about — in fact, that's all anyone talked about for the last nine months. Except me. I haven't said much. It's not that I'm not delighted and excited for them, because I really am. It's just that six months ago, about the time that my sister-in-law was just beginning to show a little and everyone began to talk babies, I had an abortion. No one in my family knows that; in fact, no one in my life knows that, except my partner and whoever is reading this journal, so they can't be expected to know how difficult this is for me, but that makes it no less difficult. My sister-in-law is only two years older than me, and she and my brother have been together the same number of years as my partner and me, so the comments we kept hearing are things like "You'll be next," "Don't you wish it was you?" "It won't be long before you're starting your family," "Wouldn't it be nice to have one soon so the cousins are close in age?" etc.

It makes me feel quite literally sick. Nobody knows that I had to psych myself up for two days before even going to the hospital to see this new baby. Nobody knows that I still sometimes cry when I have my period because it reminds me of bleeding for weeks and weeks (seemed like years) after the abortion. Nobody knows that this summer, when everyone thought I had it so easy because I took the summer off, that I was really struggling with the most difficult decision of my life. And that while everyone thought we must have lots of money saved up, we are barely making it financially because I was too fucked up emotionally to work, wasn't eligible for UI (unemployment insurance) because I quit my job, wasn't eligible for a student loan this semester because I didn't work in the preterm, and had to come up with $400 for an abortion because my medical insurance disappeared with my job.

Nobody knows what a tough time my partner had supporting us, both financially and emotionally, because I was out of commission in both departments. And nobody in my family will ever know because I could never tell them, because they'd never understand — especially in the midst of this recent baby-mania.

My mother and I went out for lunch last week and while we were chatting, I was trying to imagine how she would react if I told her. I thought of all the things she's been through in her life and I began to convince myself that maybe she'd understand — or at least not be overly judgmental. But just when I was silently thinking that it might be okay, she was telling me that her roommate's seventeen-year-old daughter was pregnant. I asked, "Is she going to keep the baby?" My mother stared at me in horror: "Of course she's going to keep the baby — would you give up your baby?" I said nothing. She just wouldn't understand.

Maureen D. Affleck

I was about to meet my mother for the first time at age twenty-four! How could anyone in that position not feel apprehensive? (Fortunately she turned out wonderful, and we became very close friends.)

I had a unique and very frightening experience last Monday, February 10. I received a letter from Saskatchewan telling me that my mother wants to meet me.

I was adopted when I was two months old by my wonderful parents — I couldn't have picked better ones myself. I always knew that I was adopted. I don't remember learning it for the first time; it was just the way it was. When I was nineteen or twenty, my mother, after we had discussed it, got the application forms for me and my older brother (also adopted) to send to the Saskatchewan Adoption Registry that would, if our birth mothers were also registered, arrange a meeting. The reply we both received was that our mothers had not registered.

Now, four years later, I receive this letter in the mail and I am not sure how I feel about it all. The best single word I can use to describe my feeling is "rush." It isn't necessarily a good feeling, and it definitely isn't bad, but confusing. In my mind, I have created this image of a woman, probably more like a friend than a mother, and probably very inaccurate. But that was okay because I was never going to meet her. Now that I am (and I never even considered not replying to the letter), I am afraid of building my hopes for some fabulous, independent, career woman. For all I know she could be an alcoholic, unemployed, and Born-Again Christian who has run out of money so she needs another source. Maybe if I prepare for the worst, I won't be disappointed.

What will she look like? What will I call her? What do you say to your mother the first time you meet? Will we immediately embrace and connect instantly, or will it be awkward with silence? Do I have brothers and sisters? A father? Who is he? Where is he? What is he?

There is, of course, also the matter of telling my parents. They have always been supportive of my pursuing the available routes to find my birth mother, but I know that, for me, thinking about this situation and reading the letter were two totally different experiences. I suspect their reaction will be much stronger and much more real too. There is also my brother. He has always resented the fact that he was adopted, that his mother had given him up, a feeling I never experienced to any degree. I think he needs this much more than I do, and this may be difficult for him to accept and create more anxiety in his life.

I love my family very much and I know that they love me. The last thing in the world I want to do is hurt them. I know they will support my decision as they have always supported me throughout on this issue. I just will hope for the best and expect the worst.

Dana Maurine

Feminism allowed me to understand and accept the overwhelming despair I felt, and still frequently feel, being a mother in this society.

I'm so sorry that I missed last class. I found the reading so appropriate to things that I have been dealing with in my life the past few years. I especially appreciated coming across a paragraph in McCannell and Herringer's article "Changing Terms of Endearment" that put into words what I experienced after the birth of my daughter. I still trip up on the phrase "post-partum depression" for a lot of reasons, but mainly because it doesn't accurately describe my experience. Yes, I had all the symptoms of depression, and I was depressed, but I really felt the cause was "on-the-job stress" not anything to do with disappointment, or the baby, or hormones. I was extremely anxious, and tired and in pain (episiotomy and severely cracked nipples) and I had no support and I didn't have a clue what babies were about, and the list goes on!

These were external factors, not an internal mechanism or weakness. I wouldn't have been depressed if I had some support — the kind of support that wives traditionally gave husbands, where she helps him re-energize for work, etc. My bucket was empty, and no one was filling me up. I was regarded with fear and pity whenever I expressed my difficulties or complained of not being able to cope — regarded as an unfit mother because I wasn't glowing, and organized, and off to play groups and shopping malls with the neighbourhood women, etc. And these were my own expectations of how things would be too. I was extremely confused as to why I was finding everything so difficult. I could give a list, as McCannell and Herringer do, of all the things I dealt with in that first year, and anybody would look at it and say "I would be depressed too." But when you're a mother and a wife, your stress is invisible — you have no job description — you are just there to do everything!

Until very recently I considered my "depression" a character flaw, a weakness. It dismayed me that I had lost my ability to always cope with flying colours, maintain a positive perspective. It has undermined my confidence in myself as a strong person. But I'm realizing that nothing has been "lost." I still am that strong person with a positive self-image. I was just in a situation where I couldn't employ my regular coping strategies. I was isolated, and in pain, and I couldn't just get up and go for a walk, or read or have a hot bath — there was no escape — I had to attend to this wonderful, but needy baby and I had to spend all my time learning how. A lot of my "depression" was just internalized anger at my partner for not helping me to cope. He just sort of withdrew, I guess he was experiencing something similar to me, but he had the advantage of being able to escape which I resented. I felt (and often still do) that I was a single mother and I had not bargained for that.

In any case, this experience drove home to me the saying "the personal is political." My personal experience of having a baby reawakened in me an awareness of many social and political inequities that I had managed to dodge, and rekindled my feminist fervour.

Laura Glomba

this week ...
i held my son
we looked into each other's eyes
i like and respect him
i believe he likes and respects me (it's up to me?)
i held my partner
he held onto me
we looked into each other's eyes
and we both smiled
then
sighed. we are on such separate journeys together.

this week ...
the triangle —
the three of us. three opposite directions.
negotiations ... and humour ... and tearing down ...
and building up ... and movement ... leaning away ...
and leaning on each other ... and questioning.
negotiations.
the triangle ... 3 points
of view
connected and tri-ing ... and
can be used as a musical instrument.
hmmmm ...

Terry Gibson

These days as I'm exposed to new ideas, I try not to strangle myself for having been, as yet, "undiscovered territory." I greedily lunge for any chance to learn, but still respect the rudimentary tools I employed as a child and young woman.

I found last night's class fascinating! It was the history of advertising, and I found it incredibly empowering to hear how sophisticated we are at reading visual images — and how it'd be important that kids learn early how to be critical of the images they take in.

What it brought up was linked to all my recent thinking about the huge responsibility of parenthood. Last week I was aching and weepy about having no guidance — absolutely no well-placed, helpful words about jobs, choosing a career, being a woman, how to handle pain, or learning to trust and believe in myself. Absolutely zip! Just a few snide comments about sex and men, and not being too big a slut. That was IT. My legacy. And I'm mad as hell about it!!

So I set out on my own at seventeen — the sadism at home literally driving me out — and right to this day torment myself for having made some less-than-nurturing choices.

HOW COULD I DO ANY DIFFERENT?! I was taught I was a blonde numbskull, my feelings were sick, body foul, and perceptions fucked. How could I care about myself under these circumstances?

I absorbed *everything* around me and got a good hefty dose of misogyny. Everywhere I went there were negative images and words about women — which constantly agreed with what my parents taught me. Women were for show-and-tell. They were pretty stupid, didn't smell so good, but were tolerable, given their *main* purpose.

How could I possibly be critical? You have to have an awareness of self to do that, and my very survival for years hinged on being numb, not seeing what I really did, and never voicing the words that nagged my brain.

I'm sad, once again, to see how new and exciting information always stirs up shame in me — eventually. That "What's wrong with me?" still echoes in my brain, even when I know in my gut it couldn't have been any different. If I could turn back the clock, having the same parents, teachings, and emotional/psychological make-up, it would play out exactly the same. Oh well, if what my therapist says is true, I can cry and get mad about this, and one day it won't hurt so much.

Anonymous

This was my very first journal entry ever. I was terrified that the instructors wouldn't listen to, or believe me. They did!

In Women's Studies today a woman asked why we haven't come any farther in the last twenty years. I wonder about that; perhaps because we are so indoctrinated into the patriarchal system, it is "so much a part of us, that to reject it has almost the force of rejecting ourselves" (Sheila Ruth, "The Naming of Women"). It is difficult to grasp the depth of our oppression, all its subtleties, the way it winds through and around our every thought, binding us to it.

As a child, a teenager and an adult, I wondered why my father was allowed to terrorize my family. I thought what he did was an aberration; now I know better, he had society's blessing. I kept waiting to be rescued, for someone to say, "Cut that out, you don't have the right to treat people that way." When no rescuer came, I started saying it, challenging him, telling him to stop the beatings, feed us and stop keeping us prisoners. I found my voice for a little while — but my father and the patriarchal system we live in had an effective way of shutting me up. I was repeatedly put in Juvenile Detention Centres (jails for children) for indefinite periods of time. Psychiatrists there told me I was, at best, hallucinating, at worst, lying about my father. How could I hate him? I was a bad girl for not appreciating everything my father had given me. For many years this and other experiences silenced me; now I am trying to find my voice again.

My mother was involuntarily committed to a mental hospital, where she received repeated shock treatments without anaesthetic. Her insanity: standing up to my father and refusing to give him her money. My mother still says she loves my father.

Anonymous

My mother and I have continued to deal with issues around suicide. It has been painful, but it has also secured a bond between us that is difficult to describe.

A very upsetting thing happened on Saturday. I received a phone call from my mom's partner (with whom I'm fairly close) and she was wondering if my mom had discussed suicide with me. The question was spurred by an incident just previous to the call in which my mom, in a very depressed state, left the house frantically, claiming that "nobody was going to have to worry anymore." Mom's partner and I have discussed Mom's depression before, but she was really worried this time. Anyway, she found Mom working at her office and called me back and said things were a bit better. Relief!

However, I know that these threats are not new and I know my mom's life is often filled with pain. I called her at her office and we had a very emotional talk; I assured her that I respected her position (in terms of suicide) yet that I would offer all my love, and support. I just really hope that my calling did not cause her to feel humiliated by the fact that her daughter was giving her advice on how to cope with life!!

I can only assure her that I love her and that I'm not judging her. I feel really down!!

Elaine Dornan

Recognizing and admitting my own racism has been a bitter and difficult process for me. I work on it constantly.

The issue of racism is something I grapple with on an ongoing basis. Because my children are perceived as children of colour, their daily life experiences are different from mine. What happens to them, what is said to them, and what they think and say about their experiences challenges them and me constantly. As a white woman loving and raising children of colour, I feel the artificialness and stupidness of defining people as other because of a physical characteristic. In the college course "Race and Ethnic Relations in Canada," the instructor, Barbara Binns, showed us that the concept of Race is a lie. Yet we are surrounded by it and immersed in it in this society. Sometimes I feel like RACE and RACISM, including my own, will take my children from me.

When we are out in the city, little old ladies stop us and comment about the girls. They ask me two questions over and over and over again; "Are you babysitting? No, well, then are they adopted?" They ask these questions in front of my daughters, never considering the damage they might inflict. My daughters have heard those two questions repeatedly their entire lives. I wonder what effect they will have on them? Ashley has asked me if it is okay for me to love her since I'm white and she's kind of beige (her definition of her skin colour). I love them as hard as I can without smothering them, and I think I have a warm, open, secure and stimulating relationship with my children and I hope that this will be enough for us all to grow up and blossom in a racist environment.

Gloria E. Roque

Una tertulia — a very vital and special gathering.

I've spent the weekend catching up with my letter writing. It has been a good weekend. I get all nostalgic when I write home — El Salvador. I get homesick. I keep in touch with two women cousins who are about my age. They keep me posted on the goings-on with my family in my country. I miss them both.

Like a woman said in the video that we made for class, family in my culture, like hers, is not just the nuclear family but the extended family. I miss my culture, my language, my people. My Latin friends and I got together and talked about home and family — that was quite the emotional gathering period. These aspects of ourselves are all of who we are. The family, culture, language, give us our strengths. They make us who we are. Our strengths are very much what are needed if we are to get together and try and change society by ridding it of Racism — institutionalized, individual, etc. We have to all work together and fight this monster which we call Racism.

Leslie Rene Lo

I was glancing through *Awakening Thunder: Asian Canadian Women* and started to read "Letter to my mother" by C. Allyson Lee. Before I knew it I was in tears. This is the letter that I have mentally been composing over the past six years since my own mother's death. These are the words that I have been so desperately searching for. Simple, sweet, truthful, painful — Real Words.

I started to wonder: Do all daughters feel the same ways as me and Allyson? Maybe this is the generic guilt letter that we all have inside. Or is there this sameness because both our moms were Chinese. It makes me wonder about silent mother/daughter relationships in Chinese households. It makes me feel better knowing that I'm not the only one who carries around uncomposed letters in her head. It makes me feel better knowing that it's okay to compose thoughts and feelings that have gone unheard for so many years.

Today I started my own letter.
Dear Mom ...

Jackie Lynne

I wrote this piece to reaffirm the love I have for the mother/woman who birthed me.

I read "Letter to my mother" by C. Allyson Lee and felt myself cry inside. The story makes me think of my own mother who is still living. She's sixty-four years old and has come through so much hardship in one single lifetime, and she has survived. One of my desires is to be able to spend at least another ten to fifteen years with her. One of her wishes is to live long enough to see me graduate university. And here I thought she took no notice of my need to complete my education. She's getting older and more tired, it seems, almost with each time I see her.

She never came to develop her gifts to their full potential, either, Hard times, closed doors and the men in her life who tried to break her spirit. My mother is an artist who has the amazing spatial ability of looking at objects and how they fit themselves together. I'm always impressed with that skill — I lack it utterly. I once asked her if she could do her life over, what would she have liked to become. She looked at me and said, "I'd like to have been on stage, acting." I never knew that about her.

I once had a dream that a cousin of mine who has been dead some twelve years came to visit me. She told me that she had to walk back through her life when she reached the other side. I asked what had she most regretted about her relationship with her mom and she said, "I never really knew her."

Even though, throughout the years, my closeness to my mother has resembled enmeshment, she has always *tried* to make herself visible to me. There are many, many ways I feel blessed by having known her.

One time I asked her if she was afraid to die. She said, "Yes, in a way, because I'm not sure how you'll be." She had held me through the grieving of an ending of a relationship a couple of years prior to this time and she worried for me. I told her that "I wouldn't be spared any of it; that I would probably for a time be very sad and that I would miss her like hell."

She looked at me and said, "Just know that from wherever I am, I'll still be holding you."

Pearl Kirby

Rain, rain go away, come back another day.... Do you know it's been raining for six days? Pouring buckets and buckets of rain. Last night I talked to my sister on the phone. She was telling me what a rotten week she's been having. She has the flu, her baby has the flu and is throwing up, her husband has the flu and I can hear him in the background throwing up. My sister picked our mother up at the hospital on Monday — they gave her too much morphine and she threw up in my sister's car. The company car. My sister sounds annoyed. I laugh. She also tells me she broke the hatchback window in their other car, while she was loading groceries. The second broken window in four months. She cried all the way home, not because of the broken window, but because she was afraid her husband would yell at her. She's always afraid of him yelling at her.

My sister tells me again about her student, the one she has to fail. And about the student's domineering father — who insists she is trying to sell them "extra lessons." My sister is sure that, if she were a man, the father wouldn't question her decision. She sighs: "Life sucks. Everyone throws up on you, then you die." We both laugh. My sister is also sick, but she's expected to take care of everyone else. I feel guilty because I'm phoning for a favour. I want something too. She tells me even though she's sick she'll find an hour somewhere to help me. I doubt it. If she gets an extra hour anytime, she'll probably fall asleep. She doesn't get much sleep these days, she's so busy working and taking care of her family.

I tell her I've had a bad week as well. Money problems as usual. I'm the typical starving student. I worry about my loan. I need a car (like I can afford it) so I can get a job. If I can't get a driving job, I'll have to go back to being a domestic. A humiliating job with ridiculous pay. I live with my mother. She needs to be in a nursing home, but we can't afford it. We both sigh. Life sucks, then you die. Ain't it great to be a woman? The sad part of this story is that I have just described two very common lifestyles for women.

We talk for hours about our troubles, just like the rain — on and on — buckets and buckets, sometimes it seems like it will never end.

Believe it or not I wasn't depressed when I wrote this piece – I was simply stating the facts — the reality of women's experience. You'll be glad to know my sister finally left her husband. My niece is now six; she drew a picture of me the other day and gave my likeness long hair. When I saw it I was perplexed because I have short hair. When I asked her about it I laughed because she said she wanted the picture to look more "like a girl." Obviously the cold fingers of patriarchy have begun to probe her sweet mind. As for my mother, she finally found a nursing home; unfortunately she doesn't appreciate being in a controlled environment and manages to run away at least twice a year. We now refer to her affectionately as "granny on the lam."

BODY AND IMAGING

THE MYTH THAT THERE IS a separation of mind and body, intellect and emotion, has endured for centuries in Western culture. This dualistic hierarchy of mind over body has prevailed through Eurocentric male ideology and the physical and psychic suppression of women. "Woman," as opposed to "man," is nature, body, sexual, animal. Tamed, she is a great ornament and slave, but never to be trusted, for, in her untamed state, she may coax the reason out of man.

Women's bodies, both physically and metaphorically, are the sites of patriarchies' strongest controls. These systems — prescriptions and prohibitions about how women should look and act, or what space they are allowed to occupy — are hierarchically organized and impact differently on women from black to white, south to north, working class to dominant, old to young.... Women's bodies, however, are also the sites from which the greatest challenges and subversions are made. The sections Sexuality, Violence against Women and Body and Imaging are all interconnected and form a triangle which has to do with the varieties of ways we name and struggle against these pervasive controls.

In Body and Imaging, several women write about eating disorders stemming from internalized and impossible ideals of feminine beauty, while another woman writes of her inability to eat because of her overwhelming physical memories of early sexual abuse. Several pieces focus on how the author looks, how that look is received and her level of comfort with it. Many pieces are celebratory in defiance of stereotypes and internalized misogyny.

What all these pieces have in common is that they question prescriptions of body and image — and nudge the barriers that prevent women from being body and mind. Within this section, although not all women's issues surrounding the body are represented, some of the larger systemic sources of oppression are named rather than laying the blame on the individual. Together, these pieces speak of resisting control and refusing to accept that woman is singular, and only body.

— *DANA*

Anonymous

driving to school, processing, integrating, flashes of insight — will i lose them? i look in the rear-view mirror and see such a look of concentration, deep frown.

who is this? memories ... don't frown — you'll have ugly lines. you are so pretty, don't frown. and I just couldn't help it! intensity, concentration, straining to "see," to understand.

lots of lines — frown lines from trying to "see," laugh lines, lots of little crow's feet walking around my eyes, from laughing, lines from living in the sun, australia, brilliant blue-skied sydney, days on the water, canoeing, paddling quietly, almost delicately in the clear river water, amphibian, with scales and webbed feet and hands, a water-baby.

lines and lines of memories, of fullness, of feeling, of living and being me.

this frown in the rear-view mirror is one part of me. a big part right now, but just a part.

and the face i wore in india a year ago, smooth fresh, radiant, is another — it's the face i prefer but doesn't seem to fit this neck and shoulders so well right now.

nine million women murdered over three hundred years. it's hard to digest. i keep burping.

Suhasine Hansen

I found the class discussion about women in the media to be a very pessimistic portrayal of women's lives, but unfortunately a lot of it to be true. As I look at my peers, parents and other family members, there are numerous examples that prove many of the points. For example, my mom trying to lose weight, my sister feeling like she won't fit into school without designer clothes, my father's fetish with going to the gym to stay in shape, and my brother just wanting to fit in — it's hard enough for him to have cancer, then to be judged on top of it by his appearance. It is a hard experience to endure. I think we are all victims of the media, from race to sex, to height to weight, to other forms of appearance, etc. The race keeps going and many suffer from it.

Jennifer Conroy

This is on the cover of a tape case that i made this summer when i got into lifting weights. My friends see it and they don't understand how a woman can be tough and dangerous, and feminine. They think the title is sheer bravado. I tell them i'm reclaiming the words.

MACHA

tattoos
leather
big
black
bikes

biceps
sweat
muscle
strength
birthright

tough
outspoken
dangerous
feminine
woman.

What pisses me off is the stereotypes, especially when lesbians laugh and agree about them. The majority of women i know don't drive trucks, or wear plaid, or own dogs that are part wolf. We don't all look like Sinead O'Connor, nor are we all baldish vegetarian radicals. Some of the women i know are sensual, intensely feminine, delicate, and also strong, opinionated and domineering. None of these is the ideal, or the end of the list. Lesbians piss me off when they insist that we are all, by definition, homogeneously political. Sure we are, from a heterosexual perspective, in that we affront their ideas, but to me i'm just me. I don't wake up each morning thinking, "Oh, what a deviant i am!" Women bring up k.d. lang and say, "about time!" as if she were obligated to anyone else besides herself. Lesbianism is a continuum. In my more flowery moods, i think that lesbians are the pioneers of love, new femininity, and completeness of self.

Michelle Elizabeth Neilson

For years my Best friend and I suffered in silence about our eating disorders. Now we're battling them together. Everything to do with body image is still a very "hot" issue for me.

I'm sitting in the cafeteria right now, thinking about eating disorders. Our group presents today. At the moment I am so furious I'm almost shaking. Women are so cruel to each other when it comes to weight and beauty. I know in the past I have been just as guilty. But I'm sick, I've had it. These two women sitting beside me saw their classmate coming towards them. They call her over to them and, before she reaches the table, one woman says to the other, "She is so thin it's nauseating."

It's extremely unfortunate, and also *not* accidental, that women, instead of fighting together against patriarchal ideals of the female body, pit against each other and degrade each other. We have so internalized this beauty criteria that we also judge our sisters according to the slenderness of their thighs and the size of their breasts.

I was sick this week also because my mother told me a secret she had kept for sixteen years. She had breast implants. She too has been terribly afflicted by personal body-image problems. For years she had despised herself for having extremely flat breasts. The tragic thing is that she's had breast cancer three times and still has one silicone breast.

Anonymous

This entry was my first written attempt to explore the roots of a lifelong eating disorder which has now led me to (for the most part!) heal it.

I've been thinking about my eating problem this week and trying to really explore what is going on there. I wake up hungry — as soon as I feel the first pangs of hunger, these pangs immediately disappear and I don't feel hungry. By the time I get to the kitchen, the sight, smell and thought of food makes me physically sick. I try to eat anyhow, but I can't. So I've noticed this pattern, but I decided to pay attention to what happens between the pangs of hunger and the repulsion of food. And I discovered that during those moments I'm thinking about my dreams.

For example, I dreamed the other day that I saw my "ex-husband" (I was married in 1988) in a bar but just pretended to not see him and ignored his presence. Then I realized this replicated the night before, when I was really at a bar and just ignored and pretended not to see an ex-lover that I'm angry at. Then I remembered on my way down to the kitchen that whenever my father emotionally abused us my mother told us to ignore him and used to teach me how to go numb. So I was thinking that I ignore, deny and go numb now whenever there's a difficult situation. Finally, I had a flash of being abused at three years old (sexually). So all this happens between waking up with hunger pangs to being repulsed by food when I'm in front of it.

Possible connections:
• denying myself food and denying myself feelings — interconnected.
• not wanting anything in my body (stemming from penises in my body as a child) — carries over to even not wanting food in my body.

So — these are some of the ways violence against women has affected me on a daily basis years after the abuse.

Sima

When I first started writing "journals" for my Women's Studies course, I perceived it as an obligatory and meaningless assignment. Soon, however, I came to realize that journal writing, and all the elements associated with it, had a profound effect on my life. One of the elements, without which I could not nearly benefit from journal writing, was the kind of comments my instructors gave me regarding my journals. The supportive responses I've received from my instructors helped me start digging inside and discovering a whole world of beauty and sensations within me. I'm still in the process of discovering more and more untouched treasures about myself.

When I am down, I feel lots of anguish in my abdomen; I feel a pungent pain in my heart. In my chest, pain spreads all over and inside me. This internal pain stirs a compulsive physical motion in me.

To relax the internal stirring of ache and turmoil, I have to do something. My hand and mouth need to be involved in some kind of activity. My mouth craves for inhaling some toxic substance, a cigarette. My hand is impatient and cannot wait to grab a cup of coffee. Smoke and coffee are inhaled and drunk with the hope of calming down the rebellious organisms, the heart and the stomach. I smoke and drink more, so that I gain the strength, doesn't matter if it is artificial, to fight the deep-rooted sadness within me.

These substances, however, were traitors. I realized that by drinking and smoking I only fueled the internal turmoil. I deployed some external forces to bring about peace and calmness. They, instead, served as betrayal agents, provoking endless chaos. The end result of excessive smoking and drinking left my eyes open during the nights; left my nervous system naked and oversensitive during the days; and made my hands overactive to grab more and more cigarettes, coffee and beer; and finally the flame of rage within me kept burning.

Anonymous

"Bulimia: Overcoming the Binge–Purge Syndrome" has been cancelled. I'm soooo disappointed — that I should not have this opportunity to learn and share. But my heart breaks for the hundreds of practising bulimics who saw the ad in the UBC Continuing Education brochure and could not/would not participate.

Registering in this workshop necessitated an acknowledgement of bulimia — it required "coming out" and recognizing we need help, or more help to deal with it. What stopped them? Pride? Shame? I understand .... seventeen years of shame prevented me from ever telling anyone that I was bulimic.

It has been three years since I was "actively" bulimic — since I vomited at least once a day, with very few days' grace. And yet it is only so recently that I know that vomiting is no longer an option, that I just couldn't do it anymore.

And with that realization, such an immense empowerment! To be free and so proud, and compassionate. To remember my last attempt at university twelve years ago, my obsession with food making it almost impossible to get assignments done. Assignments with no personal commitment, no joy.

The joy, the enthusiasm, the sense of wholeness, my journey, my spiritual unfolding, my confidence, my power, my radiance ...

And times of such sadness, grieving for the time lost, wandering in the wasteland of addiction.

Healing this wound of addiction, painful and transformative. The very wound that drained my life is the greatest source of healing ... from the depths to the heights.

Laurie Schuerbeke

The Women's Studies courses have had an impact on my journal entries. I began to articulate my inner world within a feminist context. I no longer blamed myself (as much) and instead began questioning my outer world, the patriarchy and its influences on me.

I enjoyed very much the introduction to *Never Too Thin* by Éva Szekely and I think the reason being that I too have been on that dead-end pathway of "the relentless pursuit of thinness." I always rationalized my need to be physically attractive by believing that if my body is firm and thin I feel good, and hence, my life is good. In reality, my life is real good and has been, but I have not always felt my body shape is good. As a result I have separated the two: my body and my mind. This has caused some internal conflict and frustration with who I am and what are my capabilities.

The article pointed out a very important concept, that is, the transformation of our relationships to the body. For myself and my experiences I most definitely need to rediscover my body — no longer an extension of the self for others to enjoy but my own beautiful vehicle for all the dreams I have yet to experience. In this society there are myriad elements influencing women on how they should look, and as I grow older (and wiser) they appear less and less appealing (I can go into a grocery store and not even glance at the magazines such as *Vogue, Elle,* etc.). That in my own sense is a great beginning in my efforts to listen to *my body my mind,* which is unique and on its way to being whole.

Leah Minuk

This piece grew from my journal writings on women and body image — what the world expects of women, what we expect of ourselves, the incredible gap between expectation and reality, and the resulting damage to the hearts and bodies of women.

My assignment for the group presentation was to explore fat women and job discrimination in North America. After many hours of searching, I came up with three pages on the subject from England. Once again the most visible of us remain invisible.

As my original topic turned out to be impossible without doing preparation for a more suitable thesis, I have chosen (with my group's encouragement) to tell a story — my own.

I read the surveys the women in this class kindly filled out. I read the three books I could find on women and fat. I talked to friends. I read the one available article by Crandall and Bienat. It states "Anti-fat attitudes seem to be based on ideology and not on one's own weight situation: Anti-fat attitudes are virtually unrelated to one's own degree of fatness." It appeared to me that this is not just an issue of fat — that it is about the fear and hatred of the female form, about women's self-hatred and about how the world around us feeds that fear. This is also about women's fear of losing control of their bodies and their lives. The oppression of fat women is an extension of the world-wide oppression of all women. Fat women are seen as out of control, lazy, helpless and very, very sad. We do not fit the modern media vision of the perfect female form — the very vision that makes many women fear fat, and even become fat.

As I was reading and listening, I remembered being ten years old, the first girl in my class to "develop." With budding breasts and rounding hips, I suddenly became "fat." The boy I admired called me "fat pig" in front of the whole class. My uncle, an ally I loved dearly, commented on and poked at my body. "You should be wearing a bra" he'd boom. I was. When he ran his angry eyes over me, they criticized. He'd pat my bum, he'd poke my breasts. Humiliation.

My mother's response to my blossoming body was to put me on a diet — no food from lunch to dinner. I remember being so hungry I would cry. But it had to be done! The women I admired were all so SKINNY! Twiggy, Agent 99, Diana Ross, Cher, Barbie. For the first time I realized this body I was in was wrong. I was fat, I was ugly. The solution was to become very small, even invisible.

As a teenager, my main goal in life was to not be fat. The pictures in my father's *Playboys* showed me clearly how a woman was to look (tall, thin, hairless and blonde) and what women were for — access by men. I knew that was true, so many had touched me without asking. Someone always seemed to be watching and judging. The teenage boys would run their eyes up and down me, trying to decide if I was worthy of being asked out. Diets. Salad diets, diet-cola diets, one-meal-a-day diets, no-food-at-all diets. No matter what I did, my breasts were always too big, my thighs too wide and my knees too fat. Dieting isn't enough — if they saw you eat, they *knew* you were fat. The answer: eat all the forbidden things at night, in your room! No one would see me eat and I could fill up the hole in my heart at the same time. My mother did this, so why couldn't I?

I left home at seventeen, got a room, got a job. On the street I was a walking target "Hi baby!" "Nice tits!" I got picked up a lot, got used to a lot and got real tired of it all. What did they want with this ugly, fat girl anyway?

When I was nineteen, my partner and I settled into domesticity. Nicely isolated, I relaxed for a while — until the relationship started to crumble. What could I do to keep her? What would make her love me? "Well, I'd probably like you if you were thinner," she said. I should have known — too fat, too female! Breasts too big, belly too round. I started over again with coffee diets, veggie diets, powdered-shake diets, eating the good stuff when no one was looking. And I got pregnant. Oh what a glorious thing! I could be as big as I wanted to be! I could eat whatever I wanted, whenever I wanted. Everyone knew that a pregnant woman was eating for two. Even my mom said I could eat. People brought me food as gifts. Men left me alone. No comments, no pokes or pats. I was fulfilling my role as a woman — repulsive but respected. So I ate — when I was hungry, when I was lonely, when I was sad, when I was scared, when I was angry, when I hated myself, and when I was bored. Guess what?

This time I really did get fat! You see, when I look at old photographs I discover that:

— I was not fat at ten
— I was not a fat teenager
— I was not fat at seventeen (I weighed 105 pounds)
— I was not fat at twenty-six (I wore a size 10 dress).

It is clear from these pictures that it was not fat that was the problem, it was my female form, my 36C breasts, my rounded stomach, my soft thighs. These had been my enemy, these equal fat in the eyes of North America. Full breasts must be contained, soft thighs must be hardened, round bellies must be flattened. Womanhood is dangerous and must be controlled, reduced, hidden.

I am fat now. I have healed a lot of old wounds and am stronger than I have ever been. I am content with my body until my mother says "You really should lose weight," or until I try to buy clothes I can afford. I am only unhappy with who I am when I let the world tell me what I should be. So, I ignore the media and my mother. I ignore the children who call me "fat slob" when I ask them to stop banging their soccer ball against my living-room wall. I ignore the disbelieving looks I get from women when I say I don't like chocolate. I don't usually "secret-eat" at night anymore. I don't usually eat when I'm not hungry anymore. I go swimming and walking whenever I can, and making love is great exercise. I dance with abandon and wear my shirts with the top button undone. For a while I bought into the books that said "when you improve self-image you will automatically lose weight." After two years of feeling just fine, and weighing the same, I decided to ignore that one too. Sure it would be great to be thinner, but I am not going to let that image rule my life. "Fat, dirty, ugly, stupid" have been replaced with "fat, juicy, smart, loved and loving." I am the woman I was meant to be.

Anonymous

Learning with and through my daughter, for both of us.

I found it very interesting that my six-year-old daughter's drawing depicted her emerging sexuality before the demise of stick figures. When I questioned why this woman had two vulvas, she replied, "One was for pee and the other made you feel good." I was so happy she would share this with me, I didn't remind her of the correct terminology.

I couldn't help reflecting on how differently my mother handled my growing awareness of my body. It was met with silence. The silence effectively shamed me. "Nice girls don't explore their bodies." I never saw my mother naked, much less my father. So I learned about bodies behind tents we built with neighbourhood children. Sex was never discussed in our home. When I was ten, I got my period, totally ignorant. I was quietly taken to the bathroom and given a belt, pad and little booklet.

My mother was so painfully uncomfortable with her own sexuality, she just could not deal with mine. This reflection confirms the progress we as women have made, however far we have to go. With my own awareness and available knowledge I am confident my daughter will have a different experience. With her open curiosity and natural response, perhaps I too can learn from her.

Gina Marina Cifuentes Faena

Ovaries, lots of ovaries, my daughters have ovaries and so do I. These precious ovaries, small in babies, growing in children, working every month in women. Thinking that my daughters will start to menstruate in the next two years. Oh poor Yolanda, everyone says, she's growing up, her time is coming soon. I will say, "Oh how lovely Yolanda, a cause to celebrate, to mark an occasion so beautiful in life." Yes we will celebrate, a toast, a special dinner, a hug and kisses to celebrate her warm blood flowing. She will be shown that menstruating is a delight, not dirty, not to be talked about, *it* will not enter our minds. I'll try my best, I'll be working against, as usual.

Looking at women different these days. Look at their hands, all those warm and doing things hands. Holding hands, washing hands, changing hands, gesturing hands, hands in pockets, hands helping their children with buttons and laces. Children looking at those hands that find the right holes for the right buttons, do up shoelaces like they are flying like birds. Such ease, such quickness, so smooth. Old hands, girl's hands, my hands. Working hands.

Anonymous

VAN DER HOOP DECISION — *November 1989*

The women gathered three days after Vancouver media reported that county court judge Peter van der Hoop gave a suspended sentence to Delbert Leeson, 33, who admitted to sexually abusing the girl.

The judge stated," the circumstances are unusual, in part, because it appears that this three-year-old girl was sexually aggressive." Van der Hoop also took into consideration that the man was "under the influence of alcohol a fair extent at the time" and that he was tired.

— *Kinesis,* Jan. 1990

At the time of this ruling I didn't know I was a survivor of child sexual abuse. I remember not going to this demonstration. I remember being scared to be around survivors. I remember not contributing to conversations about this ruling. I remember being silent.
  and scared.

I remember I was so disconnected to my body. I defined myself as a radical feminist (and still do). I knew stats on everything — yet I knew nothing of my own oppression. "It appears that this three-year-old girl was sexually aggressive."
  Now I sit here and read judge Van der Hoop's words. My mind registers it — Fucking legal system!
    — Another example of institutionalized sexism.
    — I was three and I was sexually abused.

      my body feels it — a big penis in my mouth semen
      dripping
                — face, chest, arms, hands — numb
                terror running through
                my body
                        gagging / choking
                        I can't breathe!
      the words "sexually aggressive" ring in
                my ears
                        shame / guilt
                                maybe I was
                                sexually
                                aggressive.
                                        .

                                    .

                                .

                            .

                        .

          . liked sucking
          . enjoyed it
          . liked pleasing daddy
          . liked my clitoris being touched

I
embody the gagging, the numbing, the pain, the terror
AND the shame and the arousal.

My body remembers

My mind does not

Jane Swann

RED SMEARS MY THIGH

Red smears my thigh
Streams heading to the floor
My hand rebelling against my church reaches
And parts stained flesh
Fingers dripping in blood
No pain
As I watch it splatter on white painted floor,
No pain, as my red fingers wind long twisted hair
Alone, laughing, covered in the carefully wrapped secrets
Of my sex

My fingers violate faces not even here
As they reach into my mouth
I taste feared, forbidden liquid
Voices whisper curses, mocking my lack of civilization
Rocking my unclothed body, only moans leave cultured
lips

White sheets blotted
Spots of burgundy on yellow towels
My Mother's nightmare, is my comforting home

Red smears on my thigh remind me
Of belonging to mystery,
To sneered at life

This tie prevents me from denying my origin,
Warm water, running bath, soon to wash away
The unmentionable.

Clean, I dry off white skin, my legs step into cover.
Breasts hidden, I shut the door, leaving my house ...
I walk unnoticed.
Smiles greet me on the bus, that wouldn't be there if they
knew....

SEXUALITY

I RECENTLY FINISHED the Women's Studies course on sexuality and so I found many of the following entries very familiar. Each time I read the section, my reaction changes. Sometimes I feel celebratory: much of the writing reflects the joy of women's sexuality. Sometimes I'm left feeling perplexed and vulnerable: it all seems so unfair, so unknowable. Other times the writings flow into one another coaxing me to make connections with issues I usually view as separate from sexuality.

Each entry reminds me again and again that there is no one view, no one answer, no one truth that encompasses the diversity that is sexuality. The section ripples with motion: the lush challenge and pleasure in "The great 'it'"; the jumble of thoughts evoked by a woman sharing the tenderness and strength of her life with her husband; the uncertainty and pride of the woman who "'came out' to the class last night"; or the writer who "can't even think about sexuality" because of the Gulf War. These writers reflect the realization feminists have had for many years: biological definitions of sexuality are partial, and the bulk of our sexuality is "socially constructed" through political, economic and social forces.

For a while I stumbled around, trying to find the focus, the one thread pulling all the pieces of this section together. Then I realized that no one thread runs through; rather, this section brings to mind a wild, splendid meadow of ideas, scents, colours and feelings intersecting, connecting and bumping against each other.

— ELAINE

Teaching the course entitled Women and Sexuality has been one of the most rewarding, exciting and difficult experiences of my life. The very existence of this course is an act of resistance, an opening up of a space in which to passionately question and explore women's sexualities. However, the course also exists within Women's Studies because of the incredible repression and harm being done in different ways to women's senses of self, our bodies and our erotic lives.

As we move through each course, it is my hope that we will be able to expand the possibilities of pleasure and desire without weakening the critique of danger. These two goals are not easy "bed partners," especially when each of us in the class brings her own mixture of brassiness and vulnerability, which affects how we learn together. But the cost of not breaking away from dualistic thinking that makes us see only pleasure or danger, mind or body, theory or experience is the stifling of our lust for knowledge. As bell hooks (1993) says in her essay "Eros, Eroticism and the Pedagogical Process": "those of us who have been intimately engaged as students and/or teachers with feminist thinking have always recognized the legitimacy of a pedagogy that dares to subvert the mind/body split and allow us to be whole in the classroom, and as a consequence wholehearted" (59).

The journals written during this course helped me be more aware of students' reactions to the material and to classroom dynamics; students have said that it helped them to get away from the idea that Women and Sexuality, was about some women "out there." One of my own journal entries, written during the first term I taught Women and Sexuality expresses some of my reactions to what we are trying to do:

> I feel as if I'm on a roller-coaster ride in this course. I started it, paid my fare, and now wonder as I jerk around the corners and feel my stomach jump as we fly downhill if I really want to be on this ride. The complication is that I'm not only riding it but trying to take responsibility, direct it too. What is my responsibility? What isn't? Safety isn't possible to create. Increase, maybe, through making agreements and facilitating those moments of passion and conflict, but I cannot create a "safe" place around women's sexuality. The question is more how I, how we can go into the unsafe areas. In giving up the protection of the known, the topics and parameters we are supposed to speak within, we plant seeds of a new kind of power.

— *PATTY*

Jane Swann

The great "it" happened to me alone
Despite popular opinion
I was not within thick castle walls

My "Prince" actually missed the event,
His roses still in the fields, his poetry unsaid.
The moon wasn't out ... and I forgot to wear lace.
My lips not red, no paint to bleach my face.

Yet it happened
With a great force, much to my surprise,
There I was, lying alone on the bed.
No canopy, or silk sheets

The famous it, hush, hush,
The ladies rush, and whisper quietly,
At this great mystery.
That, despite popular opinion,
Has little to do with wine, candles or violins ...
And happened to me alone

Zara Suleman

I am a little less confused about my sexuality and a lot more deter-mined to break sexual myths. Sexually loud and proud — that's me!

"Confusion" is the first word that comes to mind when I think of my sexuality and my struggle to define it. What do I want? What makes me feel good? What am I compromising for this? What do I stand to lose? These questions, with many others, float around in my head. Recently the issue of sexuality seems to be pervading my life. It may have beforehand, I may have not recognized it, but now that it's in focus I'm swelled up with emotions. The only thing I know for a fact is that it is *mine*, a possession that only I have rights to and that I define and that I give to whom I choose.

This great need to define and own my sexuality stems from subtle events to disastrous situations. One of these disastrous situations arose this weekend, between me and my current partner. First it's essential to say my partner is a white, heterosexual, middle-class male who prides himself on being conscious of the women's movement. The evening was intimate and tender but did not follow through with male-defined sex (penetration). Somewhere in all of the holding and caressing the topic of virginity came up. I announced, actually casually mentioned, that I was virgin, and the reaction to follow was shocking. My partner was amazed, dumbfounded, almost faint, it seemed. He said his shock stemmed from how open, aggressive and physically exciting I was. The myth of the virgin hit me right in the face. How could I forget: virgins weren't supposed to talk of sex, be assertive physically or be open and relaxed. Virgins were supposed to blush at all hints of sex and sexuality, coyly let the man/woman lead him/her to sexual intimacy and not mislead men/women to their sexual desires. ACK!

The once-beautiful evening hit a sour, painful note. I screamed and yelled, he felt bad, I felt bad, he felt bad for making me so upset and, at that point, I didn't give a damn about his feelings. I wanted to say it's over, I don't need this from a so-called conscious, open-minded guy. We haven't spoken since, and the evening's damage remains to be discussed in the week to come. I cannot get over the illusions virginity carries. I think it's horrible that most of them I know believe I am not a virgin because of personality, but what they do all not know is that it is MY choice. A decision I have made for now, a decision I will alter when I feel the need to. When did open-minded women, proclaimed feminists, affectionate and sensuous, have to be considered non-virgins? The whole incident along with the ideas surrounding virginity and penetration and general openness to sexuality, confused me greatly. Confusion is what I began with and confusion is still where I am.

Virgin or not, all beings are sexual and warm, tender and vulnerable, and to give these emotions only to those who have broken hymens is a shame. A broken hymen does not a sexual being make, only broken stereotypes and boundaries allow for that. I pray that the myth of the virgin will one day die, but for now, in good old 1991, it exists with a killing passion. Virgin equates prude, non-virgin equates slut, yet sexuality equates confusion. If only others would understand sexual needs and desires and realize all people, young/old, male/female, are sexual beings and will always be sexual beings. ACK!

"The lie, of a virgin mother, separate from her cunt, separate from nature, innocent by virtue of the abandonment of her real, and most honourable sexuality" (Andrea Dworkin, *Woman Hating*, 73).

Varney Allis

In a way, the course "Women and Sexuality" was revolutionary to me. I truly experienced the importance of "choosing" how to live. I realize now that, since then, I have consciously chosen heterosexuality, which I'd previously just gone with by default.

This is my first entry for this course. As usual I have to write fast because my time is so limited. As you may know, I'm forty-two, and have three boys — two of them are children and the other is my husband: today is his birthday. I said it like that because I want to show how alone I feel as a parent — he acts too much like one of the children, or a fun uncle whom the kids enjoy. And this means, or explains why, (I think so) I no longer have any sexual desire for him. In fact I go even farther on the scale — towards revulsion. So I'm desperate. I'm desperate to express my own sexuality, and desperate to understand the nature of it. How did it all get to be this way? What is it about my own sexuality that made me attracted to him in the first place? That was in the 1970s while travelling.

I feel I could devour the "textbook" — that I'd like to read it all at once, for it all looks immediately relevant. I'm somehow relieved to know that sexuality is socially constructed — perhaps I did believe in the essentialist view, but without knowing that it was even a view. I think I'd also bought the myth of romantic love too, again without knowing it. I hope this course will help me to deal with the stage that I'm in — which to me is completely tied into my own sexuality: post-childbearing, towards post-marriage most likely, but preceding some kind of new era in my life — I feel there is potential for new relationships, and renewed and ongoing creativity.

I am interested in exploring my own heterosexuality — yet I feel little confidence in relationships with men. I am familiar with feeling a sexual attraction between myself and a man — yet where will that go? Men are so different and difficult. On the other hand, I haven't had any sexual relationships with women, though I love to be with women, and find close friendships with women are the most important friendships. For these reasons I would like to know some more about bisexuality. (My sister is bisexual.) I would like to think that gender doesn't matter, that you could be attracted to anyone. But even with that thought in mind, I still find that I notice men more, in a sexual way, while at the same time feeling more comfortable with women.

Now is that socially constructed or what? Only the readings will tell me.

Leah Meredith

I wrote this journal entry after being angered by lesbians once again trying to tell the world that we're not all butch.

Hiya,

I had written other stuff, but I ripped it out to write this. I had to. I'm writing the morning after the class on lesbianism and a lot of stuff has come up for me. I never thought it would. I thought that at least I had a grip on my identity. But alas, I do not seem to. Not about being a lesbian, of course. Yes, I am a dyke. I know it. My problems come around being "butch." First of all, I have to say that I am not a self-defined butch. As far as I'm concerned, I am who I am and I wear what I feel comfortable in, and other people seem to find it butch.

So, if that's me, here's the problem. I was offended by the lesbian group's presentation and by the guest speaker. For the most part, I thought it was all great. It's just something that each one of them said. I can't remember exact quotes, but the idea of a butch lesbian being bad, getting away from butch being good, and that butch is not necessary anymore, came up. I know that this is probably not what they meant. I'm pretty sure they meant that there is more to us than stereotypes, but it didn't come across to me like that.

I felt hurt, I felt stupid that I fit the mould, and I felt insignificant. What cracks me up is that, with all the lesbians in our class, I'm the only one who looks the stereotype. I would have said something in class, but I thought maybe I was being too sensitive. But since I'm learning to trust my feelings, I have to believe that I'm not, although I do know that this has been an issue for me lately.

I get called "boy" or "young man" or "sir" at least once everyday. Both a close friend and my mother insist that I look too butch. But unfortunately for them it's who I am. I do not want a "fem" on my arm. I am not a butch/fem person. But, to everyone's eyes I am a butch. I even put earrings in for the last few days. I think I'm trying to be more feminine. But I hate them. They make me feel extremely uncomfortable. It feels the same as if I painted my face. I hate that I'm wearing them.

Of course, I have to question where all the flak is coming from and, more importantly, why it bothers me so much. I begin questioning myself. Is there an underlying motive? Do I look this way because it's what society says is strong and I'm such a fucking marshmallow that I use it to compensate? Is it a social construction? 'Cause I haven't always looked butch. I hate this. Just when I thought I had a grip. I look the way I do because that's who I am and I can handle all the shit. After a couple of years, the shit's building up. And now that I'm getting it from my own community, I feel that my strength is faltering. So I put in earrings, but it makes me sick to my stomach to change who I am. So I'll take them out, but I am still left questioning, who am I and why?

Morgan Brayton

*I wrote this one Valentine's Day after walking home through town.
It helped me to see the humour in the situation as well as the pain.*

Tomorrow is Valentine's Day and it makes me realize even more the
extent of social influence — especially upon women. I *hate*
Valentine's Day. Hate it! I dread its approach every year. No matter
how happy I am, how content with my life, I always end up feeling
inadequate as a woman come Feb. 14. It's worse than Christmas. I
walk down Robson St. and feel the excited urge to go into La Vie
En Rose and purchase that saucy, red lace teddy in the window. I
imagine trying to conceal my anticipation all through a romantic,
candle-lit dinner. The deep fragrance of the dozen red roses he has
brought me smells like love. Maybe I allow my collar to open a bit
so that he'll see just a thin red strap against my shoulder and share
my anticipation. He leans across the table to ... then I remember
that there is no *him* again this year. So I trudge past the Hallmark
store knowing that inside there are those stupid sappy "I love you"
Valentines that I would kill to receive. "This isn't like you!" I tell
myself. "You're being pathetic." I feel pathetic. Couples nuzzle each
other inside Starbucks and share a slice in Flying Wedge. What's
wrong with me?!! I want to scream. London Drugs is having a sale
on chocolates, so why isn't anyone buying any for me?! "You scare
men," I hear my father saying ... again. "Strong women are intimi-
dating," my mum always says. "But you wouldn't want a man who
you couldn't be yourself with — and you're strong." I don't feel like
being strong right now. It doesn't feel worth it right now.

Click, click, click, click — she walks past me, her high heels
sounding lightly on the sidewalk. I hear the deep, soft thud of my
feet and look down at my scuffed combat boots. "Do those come in
a high heel?" I hear my father tease for the millionth time, even
though I told him it wasn't funny the first time he said it. I speed
up, just wanting to get home and lock myself into my apartment so
I don't have to deal with this. When I walk into the lobby I hold my
breath and approach my mail slot. Oh god — there is something

inside. Oh, please let it be a love letter from a secret admirer! Coupons. How romantic. The light on my answering machine just glares at me, refusing to blink. I'd turn on the TV but I just know every show will be a special Valentine's Day episode. I'd turn on the radio but I know it'll be "request and dedication hour" on every station. I don't get it: 364 days a year, with a few exceptions, I like myself. But inevitably, once a year, I seem to be the only woman without a date and I feel as though I am incomplete. I know it's ridiculous, but every year I buy into it. I hate Valentine's Day....

Terry Gibson

Today I'm knee-deep in the paperwork of the trial I predicted here. Fighting the highest levels of government, it has been hard to document my story, without seeming a victim full of self-pity. Despite the risk, I am comforted by knowing I've put before the system another woman's life. I've also wangled my way through enough of the bureaucratic web I won't soon be forgotten by Parliament Hill.

After two classes, dealing with what I consider to be revolutionary subject matter, I feel like I've found my niche. What a difference it would've made in my life had such a course as "Women and Sexuality" existed when I was in high school! It makes me want to cry — and aware of a fleeting moment of envy for my niece and the less tormented reality she'll know. Already knows, in fact. It makes me feel OLD.

It bothered me the night of the first class to hear the instructor say "sexuality is socially constructed." What troubled me about it was my reactions. I'm always so quick to pounce on myself, calling myself a fool, stupid, thick-headed. You name it. As if I'm supposed to know by osmosis.

I was taught absolutely *nothing* about such stuff at home. My sexual abuse was all the information and values I got — in one ugly package. And, while I used to imagine if my rape case ever went to court, I could see the defence attorney pompously glaring down at me, accusing: "And exactly HOW do you expect this court to believe that you did not have any knowledge *whatsoever* of what these normal, healthy young men had in mind when they showed interest in you at this party?" And laughter breaks out all around.

It's true any normal seventeen-year-old would've known. But I wasn't an average anything. Nobody ever talked to me like I was a human being before. Oh, there was the occasional teacher who displayed a passing interest in my reading ability or something. But nobody ever cared enough to dig a little deeper. Discover why I was so unbearably shy ... or whether it was really fear.

So, the point I was trying to make is: with the incest secret burdening me so heavily, I learned this trick in my head and "forgot" it. The only thing which would have shaken that defence would've been if I *was* the average adolescent and sought out information about sex.

"Yes!" I'd say to the lawyer's self-righteous inferences " ... and this is why." And I could make people understand too. *Now.* Too crippled back then.

Anonymous

I flash to the lesbophobia presentation and tears well in my eyes. I relate so much to one of the presenters and I am really glad she takes the risks she does in speaking the truth. I struggle so much with my identity. I feel like it is such a huge feat for me to be intimate or sexual with anyone. For a year now I have been getting memories of being sexually abused by a variety of men for most of my childhood. Recently I've gotten memories of being sexually abused by a woman. The memories of the men and boys fuel my phobias around penetration and I can place these experiences in a feminist framework. The memories of the woman — being sexually abused as a girl by a woman — fuel my fears of vaginas, my own misogyny and lesbophobia. As an adult my experience of being assaulted by men reinforced what I learned as a girl. At eighteen, I was sexually assaulted by two women, and this experience fuelled my lesbophobia. Trying to wade through all the bullshit (internalized/externalized homophobia, past abuse) to who I am is really hard.

Sometimes I find the lesbian community so "oppressive" (a friend tells me I'm misogynist and homophobic for thinking/feeling this way) — I feel there is no room for doubting/questioning sexuality — so what does that mean, being a homophobic, misogynist, unsure lesbian. I just thought of Adrienne Rich's words after hearing the presenter talk about her identity mixed in with her history of abuse — Adrienne Rich wrote something about when one woman speaks the truth it makes room for another woman to. My truth feels so murky and painful that I don't even share it with myself.

Thea Bowering

not wife,
not girlfriend,
no threat;

to a woman with
a man who once loved me
not piece of ass
to hold in the morning
not enough to be me
justified in relation
to you

I am
in your small hand
in mine
pulled —
to an unknown broadening space
I've not yet learned
to fear
You teach me that

fear teaches me
to love.
You teach me to choose who.
Lead me to crowd of others
dancers, musical teachings
a cruel myth
Myth, a word that originated from the Latin, Mute

I think
(Ah, this is what a women's sweat smells like)
your ribs delicate like:
            wood window shutters
I think
of a cool breeze
            a
            (trying to be inconspicuous)
circle of space opens around us

            ours / theirs
            outside that
            a gel of others
            wanting
            (space between them and)
two women
smelling each other's
perfume

and

I am sure
I was not
born from Adam's rib cage.

Anonymous

some musings about "sexuality" and whatever. the presentation left me feeling unresolved, frustrated. There were too many mixed messages — or was it just me?

we, all of us, are sexual beings. It is a part of our lives — in the throes of study and exams, albeit a very small part. somehow i got the message that, for at least one member of the group, it was a very major part. am i jealous? probably, yes. i'm afraid that my "hot" days are over. but, i say to myself, it isn't that i'm not hot, it's just that there are so many other areas of my life that demand attention right now.

is the lady protesting too much? it felt strange — provocative posture, provocative dress, style, extremely attractive — trying to prove something? to whom? i felt uncomfortable — turned on? no, i think it was the double-talk, the mixed, missed messages, the tension.

too much tension, posturing. where were the vulnerable selves, what about those who did not speak? could they? did they feel confident, were they made to feel secure?

what about sexuality — what does it mean? being a bitch? tease? slut? what does it mean? i would have liked to know what they mean by sexuality. it's so much more than provocative clothes and body language.

i remember being stared at, whistled at, made to feel self-conscious (it doesn't happen so much now, and i'm not sure i prefer invisibility, i prefer to have my own space, but i did enjoy being acknowledged as a woman). i remember confronting men, telling them they had no right to invade my space. i remember revolting against the idea that i had to wear lots of baggy clothes to hide my body in order not to be commented upon.

and i think it's tragic for a woman not to wear what she wants because of the possible consequences — leering jeering, etc. but i also recognize that wearing overtly sexy clothes demands attention. it says "look at me, i'm beautiful and sexy." so then if a male or female responds it can be expected. of course, then i need to operationally define "sexy...."

it just confuses me. and i'm sorry there was so much tension, so little intimacy, so little trust, sharing and mutual acceptance. and i am still confused about the issues of the freedom of our sexiness, sexuality, sensuality, whatever, and its consequences.

and now for something completely different. in my class today, watching the girls, ten, eleven, twelve years old — so supportive with each other, so affectionate. we were working in the "ramp room," very different from the usual acting room — no windows, no mirrors. these young women looked at themselves, at each other. they touched each other, wanted to do each other's hair, trusted each other — sooooo neat, such an expression of the feminine, the female, affectionate, sensuous, supportive, aware, helping, non-competitive. i watched and was silent. their faces, intimate and vulnerable, accepting, reminiscent of a harem, of geishas preparing themselves and each other, of the adornment of women — really beautiful, touching to see *this* aspect of these young women for the first time. my relationship with them changed in that moment of awareness.

and it's not something completely different — it *is* the expression of sensuality, budding sexuality, in its most natural, innocent aspect.

funny how everything comes together!

Elaine Dornan

The objectification of sex-trade workers by some feminists is an ongoing problem for feminism. It needs to be addressed.

The last couple of weeks have been pretty challenging. I've made some personal breakthroughs and can now see more clearly the results of specific bits of my social conditioning. Now I just need some strategies to deal with what I see going on around me. I'm finding it difficult not to get depressed. One Women's Studies class

NAMING

a week is not enough. I start grasping concepts, but outside of class it's patriarchal business as usual — "naturally"; people look at me like I'm from outer space or diseased and really, really b-o-r-i-n-g when I challenge stuff that I see and hear.

Also, inside of Women's Studies still doesn't feel safe to me. And although I've made progress (I am talking occasionally), I'm not talking about the issues that are important to me. Like the sex-trade industry — I almost started talking about my experiences as a prostitute and a stripper, then I watched the group presentation on the sex-trade. I felt they tried so hard to be non-judgemental that I couldn't tell them how offended I was. I felt their take was implicitly, unconsciously judgmental — they talked about how sex-trade workers have "normal" sex lives; one woman even expressed relief and surprise that the stripper she interviewed was not a "bimbo." She seemed to connect her non-bimbo status with the stripper's explanation that her work as a stripper was temporary. It seems to me they dismissed and excluded the real women who work in the sex trade and their very real problems, and turned us into generic stereotypes. But I understand it probably was a real stretch for those women, and they tried. Maybe that was the problem, because none of the women seemed to be speaking from a place of personal knowledge.

Laura Mervyn

Still working on it — looking forward to continuing!

I've been wondering in what ways my life would have been different if sex had not been a taboo topic in my childhood. It was a dark, scary thing, and what felt good was doubly forbidden. I learned that pleasure was intimately connected with shame and danger. When I got older we did talk about sex, it was part of rebelling, but there were so many things we couldn't say and so much we said that wasn't true. To other young women (adolescents really), we reached out, trying to find out from each other what we really felt, but without ever exposing ourselves or our fears and uncertainties. Tentatively, we offered a tiny bit of our truth, but never the whole. If we were really lucky, we would be offered a tendril of someone else's truth and hungrily seize on it, turning it over and over in our mind, extracting every possible bit of information from it. Did she mean?... Was she saying what I think she was saying?... I was never able to say what was really happening for me, sexually. That may have just been me, but is it a coincidence that the only women I ever heard talk freely about sex talked about how wonderful it was, how they just couldn't do without? I never heard anyone say anything that would imply that they, themselves didn't get to enjoy regular multiple orgasms. We talked about the physical details of intercourse, but only in an impersonal way, how it was done, not how it felt. It possibly is not a coincidence that the labels we used for the act sounded harsh, leaving little softness or warmth or tenderness for what was supposed to be the act of love. If I had been able to really talk and to really listen I would have been able to waste a lot fewer years on the mythical "shoulds" and gone for what was right for me alone. And by now, I would be so articulate about what I want, and how, you'd always be able to tell it was me coming down the road by my rosy glow!

Anonymous

Women's Studies is not a course one leaves behind at school, passively doing the readings. It overflows into your life. It induces debates and conversations that touch my values passionately. Taking this course has influenced my relationships with both my girlfriends and boyfriend. Issues discussed in class move me not only to learn and expand but to get active in the community to educate and to bring women's issues into higher consciousness. I can no longer passively accept the dictates of a patriarchal society. This all sounds so vague. It is difficult for me to find an example.

Okay, I can think of one: society has a double standard for women concerning sexuality. If a man has many lovers, he is a hero. If a woman has many lovers, she is a slut, easy, has no values. My boyfriend did not ask how many lovers I had, he is not jealous, and he said it would not make a difference in how he felt about me. I wanted to tell him. I wanted to release my shame and feel totally accepted for who I am and my past.

During my teenage years I had over forty different men. This has always been a secret of shame. I always wanted to be the image of a "good girl," with "innocent," "virgin"-like qualities. When I told A., I felt tremendous release. I Had a heavy weight of shame and guilt released. He was accepting and, although he was happy for my honesty, did not think anything of it. He said he was happy because it made me who I am today. A womon who is in touch with her sexuality and is experienced, and he gets to receive the benefits of this. Great!

This is also what I always believed in my heart. My mother always said, "One day you will meet the right man and won't like your past." She said I had to think of my reputation. "He won't like the fact you've lived with men before." I took on the shame from society, and Mom's, to be my own. But, deep in my being, I do not regret my past. I am accepting of it. Now I feel through higher self-esteem, education in womon's studies and testing this with [my boyfriend] I can not only be a womon who is sexually in tune, but can claim my sexuality with pride. I now feel a little barrier broken down between us, resulting in greater honesty and intimacy. I feel more whole, that my truth is okay. It makes me happy to be an honest and up-front person. I do not feel comfortable with hiding secrets behind shame; it takes too much energy.

When I was younger I did not feel comfortable with myself. I had low self-esteem. I did not feel comfortable communicating as my intellectual self to others, it was easier and more powerful to communicate sexually. I didn't want anyone to know my heart. I had many secrets and they burdened me. When I was thirteen, my dad developed some new names for me — stupid, slut, whore — and that I looked like a hooker. It is so satisfying to make love, being able to say I love you with the care lasting more than the half-hour when you are the centre of desire. I have learnt, and that lesson is over, that is good.

Darcian Welychenko

How do I, a woman from Winnipeg, Manitoba, home of the dancing vulva, feel about sexuality today? After reading Deborah Gregory's article on feminist bisexuality "From Where I Stand" my dream of living in a big old house with some friends, some children and a mesmerizing array of lovers has resurfaced. An old lover of mine said I would be happiest with a harem of lovers I could pick and choose from any time I liked. I kissed him on the cheek and blessed his wisdom. It does seem heavenly. I realized the other day that everyone wants monogamy from their partners but not for themselves. I don't want to be monogamous. I want to be free to love whom I like. Monogamy is only good if you don't think about it, if it just happens. If you're monogamous because of fear of retribution or out of guilt, you're not really monogamous, you're doing it for all the wrong reasons. I'm monogamous when I feel like it. If I am made to be monogamous because of that big motivator in my life, guilt, the relationship won't last a second. I want to kiss everyone! But I can also be in a relationship where I don't even notice anyone else. It's a decision you yourself have to make. You can only be monogamous for yourself.

Sima

Sometimes I think:

If I had not told him about my deepest feelings, he probably wouldn't have had anything to use against me.

If I hadn't told him what racism meant to me and how hurtful it could be, he wouldn't have used the same means to hurt my already bruised feelings.

If I hadn't told him that he betrayed my trust, he wouldn't have learned about my vulnerable spots.

If I hadn't cried in front of him, he wouldn't have accused me of being oversensitive and over reactive and he probably wouldn't have any chance to scorn my sufferings.

If I hadn't trusted him in telling him that I didn't trust him, he perhaps wouldn't have closed the only side of him which was useful to me.

But then I become self-conscious and ask myself:
Aren't these the same fears which confined my mother in a suffocating closet of silence all her life?
Do I want to be a reflection of her silence?

Stacy Tatum

I am feeling very intent on processing my life — fears, feelings, views, relationships ... etc. So far I have found, for my personal therapy, facing my fears has been the most productive component in my "processing." So — I've surprisingly decided to join with the group on Pornography. It's what I'm most afraid of. When I looked at the pornography issue before I disconnected myself from my sexuality. By being afraid, I felt nothing but anger towards anything sexual — anger, fear and guilt. By trying to reconnect myself sexually, i.e., getting back in touch with my body, I stopped looking into the pornography issue and never dealt with my anger, guilt or fears. So, in a way, by trying to heal myself, I can see how I have just muted and muffled these feelings. I feel I have to deal with this issue for me, and talking about it with a group and learning from each other in a group project feels like just the right place for me to start.

Anonymous

I agonized over how I could possibly produce a class assignment due that evening while experiencing a state of helplessness — it had a powerful healing effect.

I can't write about sexuality — I can't even think about sexuality. I have been totally immersed and consumed by the war. I am so bloody angry I could scream — and do, and am so saddened that tears are constantly surfacing. At first I was angry only at Bush for confronting Iraq, at the events both economic and political that led to the war, at Canada's involvement and liaison with the U.S., and the inability for all to come together for meaningful resolutions.

Now I'm equally as angry at the media. This war has been reduced to military slogans — clinical at best, and totally impersonal. They would have us believe that this war has had few casualties, that the "surgical" operations being carried out have not caused death — only destruction of military operations.

For days I was reduced to total inaction, I was mentally and physically spent. My normally organized household is in a state of chaos. Now that I am involved with a peace committee, and have been participating in antiwar demonstrations, I do feel a bit better in knowing I am doing something. Still it has prevented me from all thoughts of sexuality. Perhaps that is a statement of my own sexuality, of my need to feel internal peace and safety. My physical and emotional well-being play an important role in my ability to feel sexual.

Zara Suleman

I still challenge all male gazes and realize that the challenge for sexual autonomy is a struggle for all women and that averting a gaze can also be very powerful. Try it sometime.

So far I've read the articles in the Women and Sexuality course reader once through and have reread some of the highlighted parts again. Things that stick out are lines like: "unchastity was excusable and understandable in man, but both are unforgivable and unnatural in woman." "Unnatural" was a big word describing female sexuality. I began to reflect on my own sexuality in that I have always been pleased when I am able to please who I am with. My emotions as a sexual being are not independent of my companions, and yet I wonder if in reality such independence is possible.

There are many questions that are running through my mind (and, as you know, I question a lot, but it never seems to be enough). I recall when I was younger, ten or eleven years old, going to the mosque with my family. After prayers we would visit with friends and relatives. I remember being so shy of men, Muslim men. I would never speak to them, I was told it was wrong, and proper Muslim girls look down when looking at a man. I wasn't told directly, but I was conditioned to believe this as true. Even until very recently I averted my eyes, and looked down. It was not until I stared into the eyes of a Muslim man in the mosque that I felt this strange sense of power; this strange sense of daring.

Well, I now look into everyone's eyes directly when I speak to them. I do not hide my thoughts and I am glad. The quote about the "eyes being the gateway to the soul" is true, and the power held by eyes meeting are very essential for my independent sexuality and my need to question.

Terry Gibson

*Since this entry, I'm glad my group coerced me out of my conspicu-
ous hiding. Taking healthy, guarded risks — now a regular part of
my life — has thrust me back to the fringes of a pilgrimage I was
destined for in my early twenties.*

I "came out" to the class last night in our homophobia presentation
and I don't quite know how I feel about it. Other people revealed
bits of themselves with what appeared to be great ease, but I'll bet
no one knew how traumatic it was for me.

Risk-taking. Ugh! Frightening.

After class, and during break, I felt really self-conscious, vulnerable and awkward around people. There had been a flicker of pride,
but it was quickly replaced with depression.

Why am I coming out to people? Shattering my protective shell.
Just this year I came out to my doctor as well.

I was going in for my annual and I knew that THE question
would arise. Every year for the last four since I started to go to her, it
was there. Hidden among the other stuff, put out matter-of-factly,
but making me feel naked in my inadequacy and inability to be intimate with anyone.

"Are you sexually active?"

No. No. NO! Enough already. I may never be, so will you just
quit asking!

There it was again right on cue.

"Yes," I said, almost defiantly.

"Are you on contraceptives?"

Mildly shaken, and smiling at her assumption, I told her my
involvement was with a woman.

Should I have said, no, I wasn't sexually active, because in the
"real" world only a man and a woman *can* be? That what same-sex
partners do isn't earth-shattering enough to be labelled as such.

Hell no! I said what I wanted, and she went on to ask genuine I-
respect-your-choices questions. I was mildly surprised, but basically
okay.

In class, I felt fear of only the people who consistently make comments which rattle the trust I sometimes feel there. Oh well, I feel proud again. I was going to do our group presentation without declaring one way or another — because of my fear. Instead I took a courageous step and I can't help but commend myself for it. Obviously it's time.

Anonymous

A written expression of the key words significant to my personal growth.

> Love
> Vulnerable
> Building bridges
> compassion
> trust
> INTIMACY
> self-esteem
> *strength*

When I discussed with my husband the possibilities of why I was so nervous reading out my journal entry, he crossed over the room, gave me a big hug — said "I love you — you are a special person — you're not afraid to let your vulnerabilities show."

And it all came tumbling down.

Our lovemaking that night was tender and as usual fulfilling, draining, sleep-inducing — spent. I'm letting go of the control I once needed. I'm not afraid.

We've been building, struggling, setting limits, resetting limits, falling down, getting up. We've been through fertility problems, miscarriages, pregnancy, birth, six months of celibacy — holding, snuggling, caring. Laughter and tears. Joy and anger. Life. I am finally experiencing Life.

Pearl Kirby

What were you saying about condoms? You said something about splitting them or cutting the ends? What was that all about? I think it had something to do with oral sex. You said not many people knew about it. You're right — I've never heard of it. Unfortunately someone was dragging a desk across the floor while you were talking and I missed what you said!

This was a letter to my Women's Studies teacher. The topic of the night's class had been "Lesbianism" and somehow the conversation had got onto safe sex. We always pulled our desks into a circle around our teacher and, at the end of class, dragged them back to their original patriarchal rows. The teacher began her explanations about "dental dams" just before the end of class, and a student in front of me started dragging a desk and I missed the whole thing. I know now that condoms can be cut in half and used to cover the vagina for safe oral sex, but it took me a year to figure out what people were talking about.

VIOLENCE AGAINST WOMEN

"YOU DREAM WHILE YOU ARE WAKING. You see nightmares and though you know it is not uncommon you feel you are losing your mind." (Anonymous) For as long as I can remember, I have been struggling to find the words to express both how being abused as a child has continually affected me and how living within a violent surround (when I manage to see it clearly) constricts me. Until now the words have evaded me. I do not know the woman who wrote the words above, but they speak to and for me, as do many of the following entries.

The entries in this section range from generalized fears about the ubiquitousness of violence against women to personal accounts of the damage done and the struggle to survive. It takes a great deal of bravery and resolve to think or write about abuse. That bravery translates itself into powerful, and sometimes disturbing, writing. All of the pieces speak to the writers' ongoing commitment to resist, and ultimately end, violence against women and children. They remind me that I still dream and hope for the time when they will no longer be needed.

— *ELAINE*

Elaine Dornan

I still have difficulties discussing abuse. I often feel alienated both because of the abuse I experienced and the difficulties I encounter when I try to discuss the impact of that abuse.

What was said last night in class about the importance of learning what to say to survivors of sexual abuse really hit home for me. It is so difficult to tell anyone about your experiences with abuse. It feels like you are admitting to a crime that you committed no matter how many times you tell yourself that you were a child and not responsible in any way for what happened. That you were betrayed on every level you can think of and some that you can't. But I feel it is important to talk about my experiences with abuse. To try to explain, in personal terms, the monstrous, destructive impact abuse inflicts upon the lives of its survivors. To tell other women how being abused as a child has infringed upon and shaped my whole life. How even though I have no clear memory of my life before the age of thirteen I know some pretty terrible things happened to me as a child. How every day of my life I am still trying to process what happened to me, and that I live my life not just in the present, with hopes for the future, but wrapped, trapped in the past, hoping that one day I'll either be able to figure out what happened and why or forget it (I know this is a vain hope) and get on with my life.

What silences me is the responses I get:

"How could you allow that to happen to you?"

"How could your mother allow that to happen to you?"

"What do you think you did to provoke him?

"I don't think I could live if that happened to me. I think I would rather have killed myself than let that happen."

"When are you going to let your past go and just get on with it?"

"Stop feeling sorry for yourself; lots of worse things have happened to people."

I have heard all this and more from my friends when I talk about being abused. They are well-meaning people who genuinely believe they are offering needed advice. But I bleed inside every time I hear those words. I feel assaulted, ripped open again, destroyed — again and again and again. I try to explain how their words make me feel, but most of my friends look away, unwilling to challenge the assumptions behind their words. So, reluctantly, one more time, I draw away from these friends and try to find new ones; ones who are able to listen to my story and not pass judgement upon me. Sometimes I see pain and confusion in the eyes of people I no longer talk to, but I do not have the energy or strength to hold their hands and explain what happened, to say, "Hey, it's okay, I know you didn't mean it," to absolve them of the responsibility of thinking about what comes out of their mouths. All of this is, it seems to me, one of the many ways the impact of abuse manifests itself.

Bad Girl Liar

One image that has helped me to create a sense of safety for myself is me the "adult" taking care of me "the child." This insight surprised and delighted me.

Lots of stuff going on — lots of stuff coming up. The week on Violence against Women was profoundly disturbing. "Nothing I can't handle," she said, a wry grin spreading over her face. The small one tugged at her sleeve — "Why do you lie?" She looked down at the little girl who shadowed her every step. The face was open and expectant — she knew the strong woman would protect her fiercely — as a mother would her young. "I saw you crying — no, sobbing — last night. Sometimes you can't deal with everything, strong one." The face was still looking up at her — probing: "You tell me to ask for help when I need it. Don't you get to ask for help too?" "Yes," whispered the strong one, whose voice had consolidated into a lump as dense as iron at her adam's apple. "But there's a way of coping called bravado; it's a way of making yourself bigger than the pain so that you can get your work done. When you do that for a long time, you can forget that the pain is still there."

"I don't understand. Why is the pain so frightening? Can't you make it better? You fixed the stove when it was broken, and you build things out of nothing — can't you make the pain better?"

"It's complicated, but I'll try to explain. Some of the pain comes from memories, things that were wrong or unfair that happened to me, but lots of it lives in the faces of people around me. Or in stories I hear. Feeling the pain makes me feel weak, like I have to go to sleep and dream myself to a happier place. I have to balance the memories with the world as it is, and that includes my own pain — and others'. Do you understand?"

The little one wrinkled up her nose; she furrowed her brow — and thought for a long time. Finally, she said, "No — I don't. I don't understand — but I love you very much and I'll help you. Okay?" Grasping the small hand in her own she said, "Thank you."

Bonnie

*By taking the Women's Studies course I have had the opportunity
to meet many beautiful women with similar experiences.*

The term is winding down and I am getting anxious and excited.
This term has been an overwhelming experience for me. I have
learned and been involved in so many women's issues. I just cannot
believe the oppression women experience. The power we have within ourselves to survive is also overwhelming.

Speaking about experiences, I had a phone call last Thursday
telling me that my brother was in the hospital with a stab wound to
his chest. His wife had stabbed him and she was in jail.

My first response was, is he going to live? The reply was "Yes,"
and immediately my concern was for his wife, because she is a beautiful person at heart who would never hurt anyone. The thing was,
she had had enough and could not take any more abuse. My heart
really went out to her; like I said, she is just not the type of person
to do these things.

Which left me angry with my brother for putting her through
the experience of spending the night in jail. I am yet to call her and
tell her I understand.

Zara Suleman

*Soon after this class I began working as a rape crisis counsellor. I
began the fight to have a "safe" place and I'm still fighting!!*

I'm sitting in my room. It's late at night, I can hear the house set-
tling and the creaking of the floor. "Crimestoppers," our local crime
prevention blurbs on TV, finished telling of a hit-and-run incident
against a twenty-seven-year-old woman. I just came home from seeing "Sandra's Garden" and "After the Montreal Massacre" at the
Cinemateque for International Women's Day. Violence against

Women, everywhere. I sit in my house and I am afraid, my parents only a few seconds away, down the hall, yet I am terrified. Images of "After the Montreal Massacre" flash through my head, and images of the young woman being run over by a truck make my heart tighten. Why? I question again and again the fear that society creates for me. In my home, on TV and the realities covered in the documentaries for IWD (International Women's Day). I think it would be so nice to run away, somewhere to feel safe for even a few moments, but the truth is that there exists no such place.

Anonymous

Unfortunately, I continue to read many news articles that leave me with the same raw feeling that this one did. However, I feel much less disempowered now than I did then. We can be sickened by violence against women, but we must persevere and fight for it to end.

Yesterday I read an article in the Vancouver *Sun* which left me feeling limp. The rather lengthy article was about the group of three men who have been arrested for their brutal sexual and physical assault of several women. They have become known as a "rapist team," because of committing the acts together. The victims whose stories were illustrated in the article were generally young and were in rather vulnerable positions at the times they were targeted by the attackers. The assaults were extremely psychotic (i.e., use of an axe, and a pipe for raping victims) and after reading the article I just felt helpless and scared and defeated and angry and violent and sickened and enraged and ... and ... !!!

I have so many questions. Why, if these assaults occurred over a fairly broad period of time and left witnesses, weren't the police able to make an arrest earlier than they did? Were these particular victims not worth their hastiest response?!!! Comments from the accuseds' lawyers in the article made some lame-ass version of remorse felt by each of the accused. Plus the article elaborated on how the "most vicious" of the rapists had had a very "disturbing" childhood, i.e., "bounced around from foster home to foster home" type of stuff. I understand the dynamics of "abused will abuse," but I frankly don't care what happened to this man as a child. He *bragged* about his *adventures* (the assaults) and even lured another man, to complete the trio, by his "stories" of fun. I hate this man, these men, and that hate scares me. I just don't know what to think about all this.

Dana Maurine

Learning to "name" has been one of the most important tools Women's Studies has given me.

Our last class was particularly demobilizing. Discussing sexual violence on such personal terms forced me to stop contemplating feminist theory, and merely experience the terror and anger and sadness that I deny almost every day. After the readings and discussion last class, I felt disorganized for a few days. I couldn't study for my other classes. I found it hard to believe how I had accepted, and even rationalized, violence. It had actually never occurred to me that what I was fearing when I walked on a dark street at night or heard an unusual noise wasn't generic "danger" but fear of "man." I never questioned why my imagination, when sparked by fear, always had male actors playing the violent roles. When I thought I saw a figure in the dark, it was always a man. When mother tells you not to walk alone at night because it is "dangerous," she never tells you exactly what makes the night "dangerous" — men. Why had I not acknowledged this? Why did I just assume that it's natural that women should fear the night!?! Why have I put up with it so long?

Fear of violence actually never stopped me from doing anything, mainly because my mom wasn't a fear-monger. I just never thought about situations as being dangerous — but often, halfway through my walk home alone, or when a car pulled over in response to my hitching thumb, I would be flooded with fear. Advice from teachers, parents, etc., news stories and friends' horror stories would all pour into my head and I would be scared. But so far in my life (though not for most of my friends), I've been very lucky. I've had only a few relatively harmless experiences where men have violated my "space." I always thought it was because I was tall and fairly strong, but since a woman in our class who is taller than me related her experience of being attacked., I realize it's just been dumb luck. Pretty sad commentary on our situation that *no one* is safe from society's violence (man).

Is it possible for women to create violence and fear, or is it a purely masculine state of being?

Anonymous

This entry refers to an article in the Gleaner *(the Langara Student Union newspaper) about offensive sayings on* T-*shirts at* U *of* T.

THE SAYING WAS *"BLOW ME WHERE I PISS"*

I remember "blowing" my father where he pissed.

I remember/my body remembers that all my holes got a "pole"

My body speaks:

.

.

.

.

.

.

.

.

. My vagina has posted a full time "No Entry" in remembrance

.

.

my vagina is into self-determination
and has developed
vaginismus

.

.

.

.

my mind and body have remained split as an adult. My mind didn't listen to my body and "allowed" assault after assault after assault by friends, strangers, lovers, doctors, teachers,...

.

.

.

.my throat/mouth remembers
and gags + chokes
regularly

.

.

and sometimes is
so tight water
cannot pass down

.

.

.my anus is starting to remember
+ to speak

.

.

.

I felt the pain of a
knife-like object enter me

Jab
Jab

My mind tries to formulate all
          this —— the T-shirts + the
knowledge of my body
          I stop breathing
               .

          .   .the pain of my
                    body is too great

                    .

                    .
          . just remain in
                    my head
                         it's easier

The misogyny on campuses

     is huge
          .

          .

     .

     .

     .

     memory — the massacre of fourteen women
     ♀

     .

     .

     .

     .

posters saying
          "No means kick her in the teeth"
     .

     .

     .

     .

graffiti at Langara
          "kill more feminists"

And the disconnection?split (mind/body) (which academia
feeds into)
— "it's only a joke" they say

but it reflects reality
women are killed daily
women are raped daily

The lesson I learned as a one-year-old that "my hole is for his pole"
is deep, and these jokes/T-shirts/posters reinforce that lesson and
send chills down my spine.

Anonymous

*In the fall of '91, a woman at Langara published an article in the
school paper in which she described how she had been violently
raped in the summer. Two male students on the paper's collective
chose to respond by publishing a rape threat for the woman in the
Gleaner's classifieds. A group of us (women) subsequently organized a protest where we drew attention to the college's lack of
appropriate action on the issue. We focused our protests on the
office of the principal of Langara, who later resigned over these
incidents.*

I took an article out of the Vancouver *Sun* a few days ago. It caught
my attention because of its obvious similarities to what's happening
at Langara. We sure aren't isolated in our struggles against harassment. Women are fighting for our safety across the country. While
some men responded to our march/protest at Langara by playing
music with misogynist lyrics and vandalized the women's centre,
some men in Ontario also reacted to similar protests in an aggressive
and violent way. This is how some male students on campus at
Queen's University interpreted the slogan "NO MEANS NO." I felt
sickened and angry when I read this. As well, forty women had to
occupy the principal's office for twenty-nine hours only to have two

of the seven men involved be charged. That's utterly pathetic! Maybe that's what we're going to have to do just to make the principal follow through with the meagre punishments he gave the two men who threatened Kim Anda.

I don't understand why men can't seem to grasp that when a woman says "no" she means exactly that. Why? When men say "no," we don't argue or try to say they actually mean something else. There has never been any controversy over what men really mean when they say "NO." I guess a lot of them are just really dumb. "NO" isn't a word with multiple meanings, nor is it a word for which only the educated know the definition. "NO" is one of the first words that tumbles off a baby's tongue. My little seventeen-month old neighbour was just here. She wanted a cracker but I knew she was about to have dinner so I said "NO." Maria immediately understood what I meant and gave up on her request. Hmmmmmm ...

Anonymous

I wrote this entry in reference to an article in the Vancouver Sun *about a child sexual assault by a stranger. It was the beginning of an exploration of how public/private and mind/body splits contribute to perpetuating child sexual abuse.*

An estimated 97% of pedophiles are married men with children

When they sexually abuse their own children
                    IT IS PRIVATE
            and their right (after all it's their property)
When they sexually abuse someone else's child (property)
                    IT IS PUBLIC

[PRIVATE/PUBLIC SPLIT]

"OTHER" (public) is easier to look at
— not own family/community
- result: don't have to look at self
  and own family system
- reinforces myth of danger is"out
  there" when the majority of girls are
  sexually abused by a relative or
  friend of the family.

emphasis on public = other
therefore feeds mind and
avoids connecting issue
to self/body

When i was abused by my father
    it was a secret.

When i was abused by a stranger/teacher/neighbour
    it was an outrage.

Pati Mathias

I recall being challenged in a very positive way to write in the first person with clear ownership of ideas instead of the obscurative, almost coded way that I kept a journal in my youth.

This section of the course on violence against women is sometimes very hard going for me because I have needed to dredge up so much painful personal history in order to examine my feelings about it. Aside from the personal examination, I am also taking an ongoing look at the general aspects of violence, and in particular, the part that pornography plays in perpetuating the violence.

Sheila Jeffreys' chapter on pornography is something I wish I could have read fifteen years ago, ten years ago. I say that because I have long struggled with the place that pornography holds in holding women in "their place." Despite feeling that I was definitely on the right track, I often felt that my arguments were lacking in substance and power to convince others to at least re-evaluate their stand on pornography. The newspaper article that is attached I wrote for the *Gleaner*, to honour the fourteen women massacred in Montreal. In it is described just one incident where I felt frustrated with my attempts to help the blind to see.

I attribute some of my lack of success to living in the hinterlands, where community values, are very much tied to patriarchal values and people are extremely defensive about their version of the status quo. An annual event sponsored by the Summerland Kinettes featured male strippers. This was to provide money to improve children's playgrounds. My women friends could not understand why I told them that I felt that for women to buy into a mirror image of degradation of sexuality was to legitimize our own degradation. In a truly bizarre twist, my social consciousness was seen to be in opposition to the Kinettes' noble funding of children's playgrounds.

Just recently, I have entered a profession (library services) that sets great store in opposing censorship on any level. I understand that librarians are often on the front lines, and when I have seen some of the innocuous materials that have been challenged over the years, I applaud their work. However, as a group, they extend their support to pornography, defending the position with "Well, who is going to decide what is pornographic?" Excellent question — I'm sure if the power structure was interested in striking a commission to make those decisions, their biggest problem would be fielding the hundreds of thousands of applications. I can tell you what pornography is and so can any woman who has ever lived with the results of what pornography can do to the attitudes and desires of men; often the ones they love dearly.

Sheila Jeffreys' writing has helped me to define some of my unarticulated lines of thought about pornography. A key concept is her assertion that the "discussion of power" is a critical element in any discussion about pornography, certainly as critical as censorship is for librarians. My next discussion with colleagues will likely have a different tone.

Margaret Sutherland

The time of this journal entry seems like a bad dream, far in the past. The kids and I are doing better than I ever imagined we could when I made up my mind to leave — we have secure housing, I have a good job and we have all been in and out of counselling. I really hope this story reaches a woman somewhere who is still stuck in a bad relationship like the one I had; if it is you, I beg you to please, please leave as soon as you can.

February 18, 1992

... but have you ever been admitted to a battered women's shelter? Do you know how humiliating a process this is, about the lengthy questionnaires you have to fill out, strangers asking you about your life and your troubled relationship and what right do you have to be there?

I was so afraid of not answering one of the questions right, and then maybe they wouldn't let me stay. I lied, telling them that it was a man who was beating me, because I was too ashamed to tell them it was another woman.

London, Ontario, May 1986

I came to the shelter in the mid-afternoon, after she had gone to sleep. I hadn't slept for three or four days, she was on one of her benders, and I had to keep awake to stay safe. I have known how to pinpoint the mood of an alcoholic all my life. When I was a child, my mother's safety depended on my knowing exactly where my father was in the stages of drunkenness, and creating the right kind of diversion so that he would not hurt her. But I could not always create the kind of diversion as an adult to protect myself. I knew I had to get out that day. I knew there would be worse trouble, serious physical damage, as soon as she woke up.

It goes around and around and around and around in your head, about how to get away, all the details that would need to be worked out with the welfare and the kids' school and the job and how to disappear, or how to work things out to stay somehow, or how to stay with friends until it all blows over.

The part about leaving that I was most afraid of was that it will all be public, everyone will find out. I was really afraid that the welfare would charge me with fraud or take my kids away — "not only is she queer, keeping her own kids in the same house with a dyke who slaps her around, plus she has been collecting welfare all this time as a single mother."

After four days and nights of these plans and worries going around and around, a spiral of despair, while being secretly beaten and yelled at (not really yelled at, the kids would hear, "just" hissed at and insulted), not daring to go to sleep because it wasn't safe and trying to keep things "normal" so the kids won't worry and trying to guess what will happen next and trying to placate, to divert her attention to something else, anything else, — you know, I read all the stuff about poor self-esteem, about how "those battered women are all the time telling themselves they deserve such treatment" but it seems to me in times like those that I don't remember having poor self-esteem. I never thought about myself at all. I was so busy trying to survive in that situation that I didn't have time to think about anything.

Anyway, as I was going to say, after four days of this, by the time I got to the battered women's shelter, I was not very articulate. That scared me a lot. I use my wits and my ability to talk to survive. It works with lovers, social workers, customers: saves me a lot of trouble. Usually, I have an answer for practically anything, and nine times out of ten it's exactly what they want to hear.

But not this time. There was this clerk who was firing questions at me in the middle of the livingroom; with moms, kids and volunteers milling around, there was no privacy and none of the questions they were asking had any relevance to my situation. I had not come through the proper channels. I had not been referred by anybody. I just came to find out how I could stay. I needed to know ahead of time who they had to tell and what I had to answer.

The whole exchange was harsh and confrontational. She was telling me that I would have to fill this out and that out and why was I wasting all this time asking her questions and not answering her questions to me — they had work to do for other women who were serious about leaving their abusive relationships.

She would not just let me sit and drink some coffee in their livingroom and get my thoughts together. I literally could not speak any answers to what she was asking me, she was impatient and repeated the questions, and I started to cry and she thought I was drunk or lying or drunk and lying, and she told me you just have to decide yes or no, otherwise you can't stay here.

This was so exactly the opposite of what I had imagined it would be like that I felt doubly assaulted, doubly humiliated, doubly abused, even a feminist organization doesn't have time or room for me.

So I took my baby and went back home...

Flying, June 1986
So I left a few weeks early. I got permission for my oldest kid to miss the last few weeks of school. Usually I am terrified when I fly anywhere; this time I nearly cried with relief as the plane took off. I had worried right up to the minute we boarded that she would find me and hurt me or take one of the kids or cause a scene, screaming at me in front of everybody.

Vancouver, June 1986
I stayed in a trailer in my sister's yard for about a month; sometimes it was cold and it smelled like mildew, but I felt so safe.

I found a basement apartment. It was a dump, but I even loved the orange-and-lime green shag carpet, the dirty windows, and the tiny two-burner stove.

We were so poor, and I was so tired. There was nothing to do most of the time; we couldn't afford even the basics. We slept a lot and ate and went to the park and library every day.

Someone gave me a rug-hooking kit to finish; it was a god-awful fake Indian design in orange-rust, grey and black cheap thin acrylic wool, but I sat for hours working on it, just sitting and making something that I could hold in my hands and look at every day.

September came, my oldest went back to school, and I still stayed home every day. He was late for school quite often. I couldn't get up on time. I still slept and slept before lunch, after lunch; quite often, when he came home from school I would still be asleep.

It was sometimes more than I could do to cook meals and keep clothes clean.

When I left I had also lost my house and my job, my friends, my work that I was damn good at. I had been an office manager a few months before; running a business virtually unsupervised, dealing with customers, inventory, marketing, accounting, hiring and training, firing sometimes. It is important for me to remind myself about that — bright, funny, capable, educated, sensitive women can be beaten and terrorized too.

I know it is easier to think that the only women who are being abused and tortured in their own homes are the ones who don't know anything better, who are all alcoholics, who are not sensitive enough to feel their position in the same way as you would, who do not worry about what violence in the home is teaching the kids.

But the greater suffering for me, worse than any physical pain, was the pain of trying to deal with all that, knowing that the most sympathetic response I could expect from many other women is "I don't know about you, but I wouldn't put up with that for even one minute, I'd be right out the door."

So they are telling me that this violence-in-the-home problem is not her fault for beating me, it is my fault for not handling it better than I did. This sounds exactly like what she always told me; I know it isn't true, but I can't get anyone else to listen or understand.

If you ever really want to know why a woman stayed with a violent partner, you have to ask her and then you have to listen to her answer. Her whole answer. Don't interrupt. It will be like entering the eye of a whirlwind, you can't get into the middle without being blown around a few times first...

So, for the next few years I stayed home and slept and ate and hid and was very glad to be safe and alive and alone.

Lidwina Bautista

My own experience with abuse and my association with BWSS (Battered Women Support Services) made me more sensitive to the plight of battered women. My entry is a tribute to them.

CHOICE

I hear nagging voices judging
   women have choices
   don't play victims

   You can do anything you want
   If you set your mind to it.

I hear a woman wailing
   children whimpering and frightened
   a giant silhouette looming over her
     Slap
         Slap
             Slap
   Please stop, children might hear ...
   Black eyes, Broken jaw, Broken ribs
   No education, No friends, Nowhere to go
   Three small hungry children

   DOES SHE REALLY HAVE A CHOICE?

Anonymous

Rereading this entry I realized how trapped I still feel. But I only feel that way sometimes now.

The continuum of violence. When I read Liz Kelly's paper, titled "Sexual Violence as a Continuum," it firmed up some ideas I have been throwing around for a while. I think patriarchy not only creates and fosters hatred and violence towards women, it institutionalizes it. And women are dying prematurely from the environment we live in. I personally know of at least two women whom I think died from the effects of living with a man who created such a toxic environment that the women's health gave out. I know another woman whose health was seriously impaired. I am the other woman. The environment was physically and mentally abusive for the two women who died: for me there was very little actual physical abuse, only one incident, but there was the continual threat of it, along with the daily grinding down of my confidence and self-esteem.

My parents told me when I grew up I would get married and have children. I didn't need a university education or vocational skills to do that; I just needed to be pretty and compliant and I would be set for life. Through all my rebelling (I ran off and became a hippie, spending my days and nights ingesting drugs, practising "free love," and protesting the Vietnam War) I never really questioned what they taught me. I thought my parents were pretty screwed up, particularly my dad, but I had been so indoctrinated into the patriarchal system I couldn't recognize my brainwashing.

So when the man of my dreams came along I just assumed the perfect marriage, 2.2 children, the cat, the dog, the car in the garage and the happy ending would follow. I was such a stranger to myself: I didn't recognize I had no need for these things. Slowly, over the course of seven years, the man of my dreams turned into a nightmare. I started realizing that most of his past was fabricated when I met a woman he lived with and abused for about fifteen years. But she still spent a great deal of time protecting him, so I felt unsure of myself and my conclusions.

Although she resisted, he clung onto this woman, using her, like a leech, until the moment she died; she never had a chance, spending so much of her precious energy on the fucker, she didn't have enough left to fight for her own life. Her children (his stepchildren) witnessed his abuse of their mother and were victimized also, but continue to live through amnesia and still consider this man their father. I managed to escape, although he tries, through our children, to control me; I consider myself very lucky and fight hard not to give into his influence. But when I hear him lying to, not listening to or taking seriously the needs of my children I worry about his influence on them. They tell me some of the "funny" stories he tells them in which women are being beaten. I try to explain to him their needs and the inappropriateness of his tales; his response, "You don't know what your talking about. Lighten up, you sure lost your sense of humour when you started that feminist shit." The courts tell me I have to give him access. Patriarchy gives men the power to define violence against women as a normal part of everyday life.

Patriarchy creates and fosters a society where women are kept on short leashes, living daily with subtle and not so subtle forms of verbal, mental and physical harassment and violence, or the threat of it. I understand the horrors of rape, sexual assault, pornography and all the other extreme forms of violence against women as part of the continuum of violence that defines and restricts our everyday existence as women. We are dying prematurely from an ideology that actively promotes all forms of violence against women to preserve male supremacy.

Chapter Three

WARNING:
FEMINIST CONTENT
TO FOLLOW

Chapter Three

WARNING:
FEMINIST CONTENT TO FOLLOW

"THAT COURSE CHANGED MY LIFE!!!!" Jane Swann mentions the religious overtones of this phrase in her piece in First Impressions. However, I have to say how much I agree with the phrase and its emphasis. Not only has Women's Studies changed my life, it has supported me throughout the extended struggle I have had with post-secondary education. I could not have made it to third-year university if I had not had Women's Studies classes to provide the content and learning style that I feel are necessary for a real education.

The pieces in this chapter focus on school and how the contributors engage in learning. We had first called this chapter "Oh, Yeah, That's What That's About" because so many of the pieces seemed to be describing moments of "Eureka!" The authors connect their readings of articles, essays, poems, interviews, and speeches from many different women with their own experiences. One woman writes of feeling she is "almost ready, right on the verge of coming forth." Two years later, she told us that the journals were an important mode of self-reflection, making the course content relevant to her own life and leading to personal transformation.

This chapter has gone through many evolutions. Originally, it was divided into five sections: feminism, Women's Studies group projects, crisis/surviving, school and language. We amalgamated the first four into Site: Women's Studies and retained the last as Changing the Terms. The first four all relate to Women's Studies courses and the broader school experience as women document their process of analyzing, fighting, coping or coming to terms with the complexities of the education system. Through this "site" many more issues intersect, and women write of racism, lesbianism and homophobia, suicide, abuse, breaking up and friendships with women. While the contributors write about the inadequacy of the category of "woman" in describing all of ourselves, they also note the connections that are there — the emotional, intellectual and political connections with other women in the classroom, as well as in the pages of books.

Often the material in Women's Studies is challenging and emotionally painful. Several pieces in this chapter are full of despair and reflect this conflict. To me these pieces echo what I go through when I am confronted with the enormity of it all — the ideologies and the systems that maintain the imbalance of power. These imbalances that play out in women's daily lives are made more easily recognizable by feminists and, although enlightening, can also be overwhelming. As Elaine says, "I am starting to recognize what a hard and complex fight it will be."

One of the places where that fight can start is in the Women's Studies group projects. This is also a place, ideally, where those challenges to our learned assumptions that cause us despair and disruption can be worked on with other women rather than alone. Women's Studies is a site where we can find others to walk with during our struggles for social change.

— DANA

SITE: WOMEN'S STUDIES

EMOTIONAL, PHYSICAL, and sexual abuse are so central to my being that my whole life has revolved and developed around it. The non-coercive child-discipline model I attempt with my children comes from my absolute resolve not to "repeat the cycle"; my interests in school; the work I have done; my life on the street; my alcohol and drug problems; my poverty and late start at achieving any of my childhood goals — all stem from my abuse. Women's Studies has not only helped me to survive school, it has also helped me to remember that I once had childhood goals.

— ELAINE

Terry Gibson

In the years since writing this, I am proud to say that not only can I still refrain from breaking into song in local cafés, but I'm now tackling, head-on, each barrier to my goals.

I get in Women Studies classes the stuff that keeps me alive. Sometimes cold, hard reality hurts like hell. But, I guess, that sense of struggling in unison makes all the difference in the world. And I'm really not dramatizing — or ready to start singing "We Are the World," right here in the Muffin Break on Robson. I am very serious.

A couple of times this term, I seriously considered suicide. I reasoned it out. It wasn't an immature thing — to get back at anyone, or make a fleeting statement to what few people would notice. It was a very real and necessary end to my pain. I COULDN'T BEAR THE HURT ANYMORE.

And the only thing is, at those times, I see death as the *only* option to stop hurting. When those moments passed, I had others where listening to my instructor's stories inspired me. Like the time she said it was her job to see to it, through her teaching, that we would all be alive to see our granddaughters thriving and well. The power with which she spoke rekindled my own. It excited me. I wanted to go on! I'd pamper myself to health and seek out whatever else I needed. I'd fight the urge to disentangle myself from the caring concern of friends or the fevered collides with my lover, towards translucence and safety. And they are so much more desirable. Allowing them in my life renews me, allowing me to entertain my curiosity of who I'm becoming. Will I have a baby? Will I get my degree? Can I build a cocoon of love and respect around me? Will I be a grandmother who rides a motorcycle and sometimes travels? Even letting myself wonder is incredible.

I felt all of this last night. No wonder I am tired and shaky today. Ah, Yes! A part of the desperation was linked to there not being many more Women's Studies courses to take. Can I keep it together if I'm without this influence? Or have I made enough contacts so I won't return to isolation if there are no more classes to take?

Bad Girl Liar

The healing process is a slow one, made more complicated by society's demand that women remain as children, seen and not heard.

I am moving through my life in a fog these days. This school thing has shaken me. Is shaking me. I've just composed a report on the condition of my early life and why I face some of the problems I do today. Immediately I want to change it — to edit it softer. Make it more palatable. Draw blame away from those whom I have long protected and smother my self-esteem with it. I will not. I refuse. Instead I will edit it so that the edges are razor sharp — so that they will cut the heart-strings of the reader. It is such a token expression of my experience, yet it is the first time I have recorded some of my experiences so that someone "public" will have evidence. I am afraid.

This feeling is nothing new and I resist my own temptation to ascribe it to my disclosures. I will not carry the weight of guilt for what was done to me one step farther. I throw it down to the earth, watching as the tangled heaviness of it contaminates the ground on which it lands. I fight these days, moment to moment, to find my strength, to keep moving forward. The fear and paralysis are like massive rubber bands trying to snap me back into apathy. I haven't found a tool to cut them yet. At least I can perceive them. I gather up the little girl self into my arms and take one more step. I will continue to, because my life depends upon it.

Becca Shears

Well, I broke up with my boyfriend of two and a half years. I did it after the class on Media — I was a woman on a mission. It was bound to happen, but I think this class gave me the strength to realize I am okay. My self-worth and direction no longer need to be linked into how another person perceives me.

When I told my mom, she said, "Lots of women end their relationships after a Women's Studies course!" I think she was being cynical, but she supports pretty much anything I do. I guess I just realized that this is my time to have fun and love life, not go for couples counselling before I'm even married.

Needless to say, things are much better. I've made lots of new and supportive friends this year....

Daphne Boxill

Unrequited love, love, love, and nothing but. I wrote about getting dumped. That was the big issue that week. My journal entry allowed me to purge. And for that I'll always be grateful. Oh yeah, twenty-seven, black and struggling.

World, you seem pretty cold to me tonight. He, the forty-one-year-old flake, dumped me. He's gone back to his ex. I'm just tired, tired of playing this scene, tired of always being there for myself when one of my trysts is over. Tired of detaching myself from these trysts only to recount them days later as amusing anecdotes. I'm tired because I can't detach myself, really anymore. They are wearing me down, I'm really quite sad, so I channelled my energy and cleaned. But really I knew it was going to happen. I knew it would end tragically from when I first met him. You know if there is one thing to distrust it's intensity. Intensity cannot last — oh I'm going to bed. I want to dream about other things.

I'm listening to Soul Asylum right now — I'm so glad I have this new space, it's sooo spacious. I'm glad I moved. Mt. Pleasant is much groovier than Kerrisdale. I'm happy right now, dancing around.

I went to bed very early last night. I am sad about the flake in a way, but every minute that passes the whole thing seems to go farther and farther away. For some solace I reread bits of Jane Wagner's *Search for Signs of Intelligent Life* ... I love that play. Ah well my life is like Timex, I take a licking and keep on ticking. And as I thought to myself last night, this too will pass...

I met with my group yesterday at Carnegie Hall — what a beautiful building!! We all had lots to say and good ideas for our project. A video. I'm really excited to realize our vision. There is so much to talk about. Almost too much for just twenty minutes. Racism is such a huge issue and difficult. Difficult for me because I never know if I'm being too paranoid/defensive or not paranoid/defensive enough. Okay I'm going to have my last cigarette and go back to Philosophy.

Michelle Cannon-Burley

I am enjoying the readings, but I now understand what the women were talking about, some are harder to read.

My husband was reading my book one day and asked what I consider to be a very interesting question: "When did the lesbian community start gaining control of all the literature of the women's movement?" And when I read the books I must say I have to wonder myself. I don't feel there is anything wrong with it, but I feel like an outsider with them.

Jennifer Conroy

I'm reading through this package and i'd be willing to bet that i've already read all or most of the lesbian content. I'm one of two lesbians in the class that I know of, and am feeling rather invisible. Surprise, surprise. I realize that as a minority, it is somewhat my responsibility to bring up homosexuality (no, wait, i hate that word, it sounds exclusively male ...). I suppose i should bring up lesbianism, but don't the others wonder about it as well? I mean, i'm a woman, too, and my issues about sexuality should enter their thought patterns. You know, "should" is a stupid word, and this is coming out sounding selfish. Straight women don't have to hide their choices, and much of the time I do. This class is supposed to be a place that is different, right? Right? Hello?

So far we've done some history, no lesbians there, and when we look at women and the media... Well, there are no lesbians on TV or in commercial advertising. Help, i'm drowning in the Breeder Sea! The point is that we are numerous and always have been and i feel hidden by the course outline. Should I accept that lesbianism is an abstract, comparable to "women in the Middle East," or "the struggles of women in non-traditional careers?" Do you really think that I'll accept that women (read: hets) will be taught about lesbianism only in the Women and Sexuality course? I absolutely will NOT be defined solely in terms of my sexuality! I am a student, a record-retail worker, a cyclist, a musician and a red-head as well as a lesbian. I deserve (we deserve) more mention than only when dealing with sex or extended families.

I realize that one of the major reasons that lesbian content and dialogue are so scarce is because we have been largely invisible for so long. But to continue addressing women's issues with a token or marginal reference to lesbians serves only to erase and negate us further.

Iris Fabiola Naguib

THE COLOUR LINE

Not light enough
never dark enough
they
leave me no room.

No place of safety
no place to hide.

I'm torn
but can't show it
I'm so angry
and yet,...
I feel more sorry
for them
than I've ever felt for myself.

Elaine Dornan

I have incorporated my interest in both language and history into two minors.

Tonight I developed a deeper understanding of the importance of historical knowledge and also of the importance of the language we use to explain ourselves. I have always enjoyed history and toyed with making it my teachable minor for my Education degree. Now I'm sure it will be. In class tonight I came to understand how history is vital to my ability to put things in context. Initially I was surprised and saddened as we did the round and many white women reacted with anger and confusion to the readings on racism where they felt they were judged unfairly by the colour of their skin. I was surprised that they didn't seem to make the connection between how they felt about being judged and how people of colour feel every day of their lives.

I was saddened that the white women in our class seemed to understand racism as an individual's own personal problem, not as a systemic one. But then, you talked to us about history giving us the ability to understand the broader picture and I got the feeling that what these women are going through is just the beginning of the journey for them. Most of the information they are receiving in Women's Studies is totally new to them and still needs processing. I saw hope; I see hope in Women's Studies more than any other course. Hope for deeper analyses, for empathy, for reaching out to all women to celebrate our differences as well as our similarities.

Daphne Boxill

*Race, race, race, and nothing but. A huge issue — my issue. Yeah,
I got to write, talk and make a group project out of it. Writing
allowed me to validate my feelings. And for that I'll always be
grateful. Oh yeah, twenty-seven, black and struggling.*

I want to say I am actually dreading Women's Studies tonight. I am
sick of talking about race issues with White people or those people.
I don't want that chick staring at me again. She always fucking does.
I'm not being paranoid. I talked to my friend about it.

I just bought bell hooks's *Black Looks* yesterday. I went to see
two films at the National Film Board (NFB) yesterday for my
research paper. Dionne Brand's *Sisters in the Struggle* and John N.
Smith's *Sitting in Limbo*. I went with a white friend. I should have
gone alone. I couldn't relax and fully enjoy these two films. I was
worrying about her response. The remarks she would make. I feel so
caught, stuck. We introduced the heated topic of race — as well as
feminism — and although it's great to have it talked about, I feel
trapped, surrounded by all these ignorant, curious, defensive white
faces. Worried by their reactions. I have this internalized fear.

Last term when we talked about racism I found I wanted to be
very much "even" — not too angry, not too passive. People came to
me after class and wanted to know my racist experiences, etc. It dis-
gusted me. Fuck, I don't know. Maybe this class won't be so bad. I
guess what it boils down to is I just find this issue so depressing — I
feel like a whole lot of negative energy is being passed around. I hate
having to re-evaluate everything.

Okay and yeah man. He is GONE GONE GONE. FUCKED AND
FUCKED OVER. I miss him REAL BAD. WEALLY WEALLY BAD. FUCK-
ER I'm just in a hugely negative zone right now. I hate philosophy,
my man has upped and gone. I'm tired of courting controversy, I'm
tired of the bulk of women in Women's Studies class, man, I do not
know. This overwhelming feeling will pass. On a good note I dug
Nym Hughes's article "Why I Can't Write about Class."

Okay I must put myself on BICYCLE AND PEDAL MY WAY TO
SKOOL.

Anonymous

down time — low energy — flu time. grumpy, depressed, and try-ing to just let myself be that way, not feeling like i have to pull myself out of the mire, but just hanging out in the mire for a bit, exploring how it feels to be allowed to be miserable.

partly flu, partly the mid-term blues, but a good partly is that i know i did poorly on my psych mid-term. it pulled the floor out from underneath me. i thought if i study hard and long, and follow the routine that has worked for me so far, that i'll do well. maybe not As, but a B would be fine. so i studied long and hard, and i'm not sure that i even passed.

so what does that mean? that i can't do this — that i'm crazy to consider continuing in university, that so far i've just been lucky, instructors have liked me, that they didn't read closely what i was saying, that they didn't recognize that i'm a fraud. sooner or later they'll find out that i'm not intelligent, original or worthy of their As.

it seemed like i got caught — see i really am only a "C" person — or a "D" person, or even worse, a failure.

all that because i didn't do well on an exam in a subject that i don't enjoy, that i don't choose to do, that i'm not interested in, that i have to do. all that because the instructor hasn't taught this course before and wrote an impossible exam!

i let it get me down. is my self-esteem so dependent upon being an "A" person?

so i can look back on the week in perspective, recognize that i was emotionally drained from studying, vulnerable, physically drained from sleepless nights worrying about the exam, had a mild case of the flu — put into perspective i wonder how i could spend so long in the mire.

but i'm still glad i didn't put on a happy face, i'm glad i was hon-est about how i was feeling, valid or invalid, crazy or not. i didn't answer "I'm fine" with a phoney, sunny voice.

i was just me — discouraged, depressed and needing hugs.

i just got the results of my psych mid-term: an A — i am suitably amazed, embarrassed, encouraged, proud.... how little it takes to make me happy! what a funny game we play in this academic unreality!

Maureen D. Affleck

The stress of university, and life, often seem like more than one can bear, and it sometimes helps to release just by writing down thoughts.

Well it's that time of year again. No organized thoughts here. Just a mumbo-jumbo of stress and commitments, many unfulfilled. School — always school — midterms, papers, studying, homework, reading — never ending, always behind. And then there's just life — housework — dirty dishes, dinner? How about popcorn! Unpolished shoes and fingernails. This would be a good time to be single! Time for a mate? None. Sex? Forget it! I don't have the time or the energy. "Sorry, dear, but I'm just going to go to sleep now." This doesn't go over very well. Rent? Bills? Money? I haven't even got around to November's rent yet. I just don't answer the door. Or the phone.

Next year, I'll be more organized. Next year I will start my papers early and do my reading on time. Next year I will save some money. Next year I'll get a boyfriend with a job so I don't have to try (unsuccessfully) to support him when I am a starving student already. Next year I will take care of myself by eating properly and maybe even exercising. Next year I will get straight As. Next year will be different.

But wait, didn't I say all that last year?

Anonymous

I wrote this entry when I was just "coming out" as a feminist. However, I continue to be curious about the power of the hegemonic ideology to turn women against ourselves.

There is something that is bothering me. It is fairly obvious that women have had to fight men's ignorance and insensitivity to so many women's issues, but in the last couple of weeks I've heard more comments from young women that indicate an ignorance of the women's movement than ever before in my experience. I don't know if it's the change in atmosphere for me (this is my first-full time semester at Langara) or if it is perhaps my own attitudes occupying a vivid portion of my thoughts.

It really disturbs me to hear a woman say something like, "Oh, don't worry, I'm not into the *feminism* thing" when talking to a man (or other women for that matter). I see this as a woman conveniently removing the "threat" for the man's sake. Who ever said feminism was a fad in the first place? I really hate the assumption that the search for equality and removal of old destructive customs has to be seen as radicalism — especially in the eyes of so many women. I don't understand the motive behind their words. Perhaps it's the fear. I guess that is something everyone will have to deal with in their own way, but, personally, I would be much more afraid of continued male dominance over women than of some of the serious measures that must be taken in order to break the age-old pattern. My advice to women who "hate feminists" would be for them to step outside of their comfort zone and take in the big picture because internal happiness is a lot harder to fake!

Christie Woodin

I've been thinking a great deal lately about relationships between women. In my life right now, there seems to be more focus on this and more opportunity to consider it than at previous times. Being in a Women's Studies class is part of this (especially working on the group project), as is spending more time hanging out in the Women's Centre, chatting, spending more time with my women friends and attending more women's events.

It seems to me that in our teenage years there's lots of opportunity to spend time just with other females and to develop close, strong bonds with them. But as we get older, the emphasis is placed much more on developing close relationships with men — regardless of the impact this may have on our ties to the women we've been close to for years. Although my circle of friends now is quite an even mix of men and women, both hetero and homosexual, I've realized lately that I spend far less time with other women than I did ten years ago. My partner and I together have a busy social life and spend a lot of time with other folks of both genders, but very rarely do I take an evening and go out alone with another woman, or send my boyfriend out for the night and invite a group of women over. I'm feeling more and more like female energy is really lacking in my life. It's an easy thing to let slide (for me, anyway) because I forget how important it is until I spend an afternoon in the Women's Centre chatting with other women. After such an afternoon I suddenly realized that I *need* this. It is necessary to my mental health to be able to talk with others who challenge me when I'm complacent about issues, validate my feelings when I think I'm being paranoid, understand me when my (male) partner does not, and give me another angle on the issues that are on my mind.

I need to make more of a conscious effort to make time for women in my life and I need to put some energy into strengthening the relationships I have with women friends.

Anonymous

This was my first journal entry written for my first (of many!) Women's Studies courses.

Re: *Women's Reality* by Anne Wilson Schaef.

This is the second time I am reading this book. The first time I was going through what I call my reactive, emotional, enraged stage. I felt like my world was coming tumbling down around me. I had just come back from two years abroad and everywhere I looked I saw SEXISM. My family thought I was crazy, sick (must be those parasites) hysterical — when I should lament to my mother she would say "that's just the way it is." Dismissed. SLAM. OUCH. I cried a lot. My partner at the time was not supportive. I went to a counsellor and was told not to go to any kind of women's group because it would "alienate me from reality." I couldn't deal with *reality*. I was extremely vulnerable. When I got *Women's Reality* between my shaky hands I read it cover to cover and related 100 percent for the first time ever. Everything fit. I thought maybe I wasn't crazy. What a breakthrough. Sometimes I still think I am crazy. Somehow it hurts me to hear that other women can read this book and not only not relate, but disagree.

I have been gobbling up feminist literature. It's my haven. When finally I feel grounded, centred and a little sure about reality it shatters when I speak to my father, my mother and my siblings. When they tease me, label me and make me the butt of their jokes, I feel like maybe I am wrong, crazy, hysterical and trying to create a world of utopia or framework that is "unrealistic."

Sometimes I'm scared to read feminist literature because I feel that I'll become too "radical," hard-nosed, and pessimistic. I sometimes, despite myself, recognize that I gain self-esteem from male validation. This recognition makes it harder.

Varney Allis

I entered Women's Studies as someone about to parachute-jump for the first time. It was thrilling to discover myself through the readings, the discussions and these dialogue journal entries. It was also scary and painful too, but I needed to go through with it.

I've just been to the film *Margaret Laurence: First Lady of Manawaka* and talk by Cynthia Flood, Langara instructor and short-story writer. I love both their writing, however different. What is simply *screaming* at me right now is the notion of Lawrence's — about "speaking the heart's truth" — and how Cynthia talked about the need to do this, plus the sometimes awful consequences (referring to

The Stone Angel's Hagar, who didn't until she was ninety) — how I just read about this in last week's readings — the silence into action, that feeling of being punched from the inside out.

As I drove home from Langara, and cruised down Nanaimo Street, as I do every day, I thought of myself as needing rebirth, of giving birth to the other me that I know is there — or of someone unknown in the dark, but whom I know is almost ready, right on the verge of coming forth. I thought of myself trying to explain to a friend, "You see I'm fighting my own oppression, both internal and external." And then I cried — hoping the other cars weren't looking.

Now I know why I chose senior women as my project — to face myself getting older and to do "my heart's truth" — to live my life as I want, and not as I am "supposed to" — before I get a minute older — and certainly before, like Hagar, I turn ninety. If I do this (follow my heart's truth) I will not be following my mother's footsteps, and perhaps not be as miserable as her. However, I know I must also face the consequences.

Gloria Murray

Writing is such a struggle. To just let words come without worry-ing about sentence structure and organization — that is freedom!

It's raining, it's late at night and I am tired but I want to write this entry in my journal. Shall I write about our group project, or shall I talk about the guilt I feel about spending so much time on school work and neglecting my family, or shall I just talk about the soft rain falling — washing away my thoughts, my worries?

I'll talk about the project.

Warm sun poured through the window as we drank good coffee and ate delicious fresh buns from the bakery around the corner. It was cosy there. The women were warm and friendly, and it was just a lovely Saturday morning. I sipped my coffee and looked at the faces of these women filled with dreams, hopes and inspiration.

I think, yes, life is a gift — this moment is a gift — these women are a gift — they give me a chance to see the world from other perspectives — they challenge me to be creative and it feels right — and it feels good — and I think this is the way to learn — no memorizing and researching in cold old libraries. This is real — this is life happening right now and out comes my creativity, out comes inspiration.

I am filled with hope, but also respect for human life. Working together can be quite a challenge — it takes a generous spirit, flexibility, open-mindedness, co-operation, patience, and willingness and forgiveness. It helps me to stay human — I am glad for the experience — I live too alone at times — do my work on my own — it would be nice to work together more — learn together more — I learn so much more, I realize, in groups.

It's still raining outside — I'm getting more tired — I have not been sleeping well — I often suffer from insomnia. I worry about how I will get my work done, I worry that I may have made a mistake leaving my $40,000-a-year job to talk about creative images of women and sex.

Then I think, no, Saturday morning was a lovely morning. I can be more me. I just struggle on. Maybe the rain will lull me to sleep tonight. I sure hope so. I worry about my mom, I feel I am neglecting her — I should call her — I don't want to; it reminds me that I'm not caring for her enough. I love her so — I hope she understands — I hope she's not lonely.

Oh to be human, to suffer and to experience joy — what a bunch of mumbling I'm doing — I am tired — school is hard work. I think our group has some good ideas. I think I ended up with some very creative women — that's neat.

I'm almost asleep now. Good night.

Jean Moran

In varying degrees the issue of control has haunted many members of my family. Some are healing and some continue to emotionally batter and manipulate people who are or have been close to them. I want to contribute to stopping this cycle of abuse. I needed to begin by learning to trust again, but the process has been excruciatingly slow. Thankfully I am crawling out of this pit of fear and starting to invite risk, vulnerability and romance back into my life.

I have never been good at working in groups.

I grew up knowing that the only person I could count on was myself. To rely on someone else would have been foolish, almost certainly ending in disappointment.

I knew I was reliable. If I looked after matters myself, there would be no danger of an emotional letdown. I isolated myself, but I felt safe.

Working in a group has always been terrifying; at the very least, it has been extremely uncomfortable.

I worked in a group in French to write a short skit. I insisted I had loads of time and I would gladly compose the vignette. I bulldozed right over my group members. They were very young and didn't have a chance.

In English, I was in four of a group. I was the oldest (by far) and the only woman. I treated them maternally. I patronized them shamelessly, insisting I was sure they had more important things to do with their time and that I wouldn't mind a bit commandeering the project. The guys were quite happy with this arrangement. Anything to get CONTROL. I certainly couldn't allow myself to depend on anyone and place myself in such a vulnerable position. I would have found bungee-jumping off the CN tower in Toronto more attractive than fully participating in a group project. Just give me all the work and I'll look after it all. No, really. I don't mind a bit.

Now, I'm in Women's Studies 216. And, gulp, I have to work in a group. Gee, can't I just jump off the Burrard Street Bridge with my pants on fire cleverly juggling three live grenades and two poison-tipped knives?

But wait! Something has gone terribly wrong with my usual dynamic in group avoidance. I managed to function in a group without exploding or my brain falling out. I didn't even run screaming out of the room.

Our first two meetings, however, I did not participate a great deal. I was spending too much time feeling paralyzed or frightened. We met six times and talked on the phone. As I got to know these women, I started to relax. I allowed myself to trust. I was able to join in and contribute along with everyone else.

I learned a new freedom in this exercise. I could surrender a part of myself. I emerged from this experience with no feelings of hurt or disappointment, but with the warmth of new friendships and a sense of accomplishment.

Daphne Boxill

Life, life, life, and nothing but. Women's Studies valued my life, my experiences and, what's more, encouraged me to put pen to paper and write about it. For that I'll always be grateful. Oh yeah, twenty-seven, black and struggling.

I've been sick. This weekend we were supposed to edit our hour-length video into fifteen short minutes. The machine fucked up on us, so we couldn't, but as we watched the video we made last week a funny thing happened. We changed our minds about things we'd said. Or we wanted to talk about other issues.

I had been okay I thought — that was until I watched this video my mother had sent me oh so long ago that I had never been able to watch (I've never had a TV or VCR until just now). It was this documentary on this race-relations expert Jane Elliott who did this experiment called "A Class Divided." She used it in her Iowa classroom to teach her students about racism. She divides the class into Blue eyes and Brown eyes. For one week she treats the blue-eyed people very poorly and the brown-eyed people very well and then she switches the tables. It worked so well that it expanded into a workshop.

Anyway, my mother taped her on *Oprah* and this woman, Jane Elliott (a white woman), was addressing all sorts of issues, especially how racism is taught in the schools. This is when shivers started going up and down my spine. She asked how many people of colour have had teachers say to you, "I don't care if you're Black, Green, Yellow or Purple with Red Stripes." I certainly have, not just teachers but other people as well. Elliott was saying that they're comparing people of colour to extra-terrestrials. Yes! and of course the old standby — "I don't see you as Black, or You're not really Black" — so what people who say this are inferring is that there is something wrong with being Black — a deformity that we will do our best to overlook.

So after hearing all this and thinking about it, I immediately wanted to change my focus on the video. One thing that Elliott said was that all white people are racist. I am not comfortable with that. How can I befriend a racist — or members of my family that are white — how can I love them if they are racist? I suppose the argument is that racism is a disease and they are trying to fight it — yes — but it seems so much easier to live in denial. I am changing though; I am outgrowing friends who aren't as aware — or, no, that's a poor way to phrase it, who I can't talk to about a variety of issues. Whenever you make a discovery it seems like then a million questions come flying in your face.

Like, okay, suppose I can talk to a friend about a variety of issues, but do we have to agree for me to remain friends? It's tricky, very very tricky. TRICKEE.

Iris Fabiola Naguib

This poem was inspired by and written to the white women I have taken Women's Studies with who took the liberty of speaking for me, at me, over me, through me and about me.

TO THE WHITENESS OF YOUR WAYS

Speak to me
not only
of your life
your experiences
and your struggles

Speak to me
of your efforts
to read about
listen to
and acknowledge
other peoples' experiences
and their lives

Speak to me
not only
from a place of fear
and ignorance
when you say
we are "different"
or how we are the "same"
when your guilt becomes conscious

Speak to me
of your efforts
to recognize
your own denial
your own conditioning

Speak to me
not only
of how society has been
or will continue to be

Speak to me
of your part
in positive social change
of your part
in the creation of equality
and justice

Speak to me
not only of
your socialization
your family
and why you may be this way

Speak to me
of how you fight
against your own ignorance
your own racism
and what you are doing
to grow beyond it

Speak to me
not only
of my responsibilities
to share my strength
and to educate others

Speak to me
of how you take responsibility
how you help others
and how you are educating yourself

Speak to me
not only
of how you think

I feel
or how you assume
that I must experience life
as you do

Speak to me
of your experience
without assuming
that you can relate to mine
or that I can relate to yours

Speak to me
not only
of the chosen status quo
Speak to me
of reality
not fallacy

Speak to me
don't try to dominate me
And
before you speak
at least
pick up and read some books
at least
listen to what is being said
or not said

and listen to yourself
at least
open your eyes
and face
what is all around you
injustice, inequality, exploitation, subjugation, . . .
must I always go on?
Look at what the state of the world is telling all of us
THEN
COME SPEAK TO ME

CHANGING THE TERMS

I STRUGGLE WITH LANGUAGE, trying to break through, to connect, with words. I continue because I believe in their power and promise. They are tools of resistance through which we can struggle to understand our world, deal with it critically and creatively, and through which we hope to reshape our realities and effect transformation.

The entries in this section address the everyday struggles women are waging with words; their growing awareness of the underlying issues of power and authority implicit in language; and the opposition they encounter. Even though "seeing the issues plainly and speaking up about them is dangerous," Bad Girl Liar and many others continue to take up the task: tussling with words, striving to understand them, revealing the ideologies behind words. For ideologies revealed can become ideologies dispelled.

— ELAINE

Michelle Elizabeth Neilson

I think this was my first journal entry. I remember feeling relieved after writing about the "Gingerbread person experience" because that woman made me so angry.

I was working at a bakery where they make gingerbread cookies. The sign on the cookie tray in the display case said "Gingerbread man." Funny how I had not really noticed this until a regular customer pointed out to me that perhaps the sign should be changed to "Gingerbread person." I thought about it and decided this was a good idea because the little cookie indeed had no "gingerbread penis" and why should a child eating it have to assume this neuter cookie was a man. I changed the sign.

I did not correct people when they said "gingerbread man." I didn't feel that the point needed to be made verbally. I thought the sign was enough. I didn't assume I would get any flak for my change on the sign. One day a semi-elderly English woman came in and became quite irate upon seeing the sign. She chewed me out for being "bloody feminist": "How ridiculous, it's a cookie! What is the world coming to? MY God, I mean manhole cover, person-hole cover, bloody feminist." She then went on to say how upset she was that some people didn't think Captain Cook (discovered Vancouver) should be celebrated. She condemned my feminist attitude and several other concepts of change.

The whole time she was spouting off I imagined what I would like to say to her if I didn't need my job so badly. I would have liked to have said: "Yes, I'm a feminist. I'm also a Jew. This is a Kosher bakery. Oh yeah, I'm also Irish Catholic, a member of the NDP Party and ... a lesbian."

Laura Glomba

Thought, noun
verb. **think**, reflect, cogitate, consider, reason, deliberate, contemplate, meditate, ponder, muse, dream, ruminate, speculate, brood over, con over, study; bend (or apply) the mind; digest, discuss, hammer at, hammer out; weigh, realize, appreciate, fancy.

> you can
> stop
> and
> think. and ponder. pontificate.
> and
> i now see movement in thinking.
> move
> progress
> voyage
> flow
> mercurial ...

words are important, exciting.
placing them inside
using them
working with them
looking at them
respecting, understanding
and thinking and moving with them.

this week there is curiosity and a low rumble of desire, a
desire for more.

apprehension sometimes — anger often —
and this week it's ok. ok. to sit next to the
confusion, anxiety or whatever
pops-up.

it's a lot of information
not good news.
not easily / passively
forgotten.

Christie Woodin

On the CBC last week I heard an interview with a woman in one of
the Baltic states. The (woman) interviewer began with an introduction of the woman as a "short and rather heavy-set woman...."

Was this necessary? Was it relevant? If the interviewee had been
a man, would we have heard whether he was heavy, slight, short,
tall, etc.?

In our Women's Studies class last week, during a discussion
about women's music, one of the (male) students commented that
women's taste in music is varied, just as women come in different
shapes.

Different *shapes*? Would someone use this comparison in
describing men's varied musical tastes? How about different backgrounds, different interests, different lifestyles ... not different shapes.

At a conference I attended last weekend, one of the speakers (a woman) closed her speech with a quote from Winston Churchill that she thought would be amusing. It was a story of Churchill coming into Parliament drunk and a female colleague said, "Mr. Churchill you are drunk." He responded," Madam, you are ugly, in fact you are disgustingly ugly, and in the morning I will be sober but you will still be ugly."
Most people laughed. I did not.

Why is it that women are constantly described, judged, rated, valued (or not), listened to (or ignored), validated (or dismissed) on the basis of their looks? I was especially discouraged by these three examples as two of them were comments made by women (educated, respected, high-profile women), while the other was made in the midst of a Women's Studies class. We still have such a long way to go.

Coral Gallagher

Over the years I have received many subtle messages that attempt to invalidate my working role as homemaker — yet none so blatant as the following personal experience.

A DAY IN THE LIFE OF

A Play

Scene: A mother, just turning forty, sits in her livingroom with her year-old son on her lap. She is dressed in comfortable clothing; he is dressed in only a sweatshirt and socks. A six year-old daughter is in the adjoining dining room, colouring at the table. The mother and daughter are chatting. The mother playfully chastises her son for peeing on her as the daughter protests loudly at the grossness of it all. There is a knock at the door. The mother, holding her son, answers the door, as the daughter excitedly tries to see who it is.

At the door there is a woman in her early forties, carrying a clipboard. She has on high heels and a tailored overcoat.

WOMAN: Hello, my name is Ann Smith. I am a telephone company representative. We are currently updating our directories. I wonder if you could take a moment to answer a few questions.

MOTHER: Certainly, come in please.

They seat themselves in the living room. The floor and furniture are covered with miscellaneous toys and children's clothing. The mother moves a diaper to clear space for Ann.

ANN: Please, go ahead and finish diapering him.

MOTHER: Oh no, that's okay I was just airing him out a bit. Besides he likes to play with his penis.

DAUGHTER: My mom doesn't mind if he pees on her.

ANN: (looking down at her form): You are Coral Gallagher?

Coral confirms.

ANN: I have a Barry Truter listed at this address as well. Is he your ... let's see, how should I put this?

CORAL: He is my husband, yes.

ANN: Fine ... so he is the head of the household.

CORAL: No, I would say I am the head of the household.

ANN: (dubiously): Yes, I see. Your occupation then?

CORAL: I am a homemaker. I work in the home.

ANN: But do you work outside of the home?

CORAL: No.

ANN: So, then, you are not working.

CORAL: Yes, I work in the home.

ANN: I only have space for "working," in which case I need the name of an employer, or "not working."

CORAL: Do you have a space for "self-employed?"

ANN: Mrs. Truter, I can't put you as head of the household if you are a homemaker.

DAUGHTER *(interrupting)*: She's not Mrs. Truter. Her name is Gallagher. So is mine. Shavawn Leona Gallagher. My brother is a Truter, though. He's Duncan Evan Gallagher Truter.

ANN: That must be confusing.

CORAL: She doesn't sound the least confused to me. Now if you'll please excuse us.

Coral leads the way to the door and Ann exits. Coral watches Ann from the window. As Ann reaches the end of the walkway, she begins to furiously erase what she has written on her forms.

Shavawn: What are you doing, Mommy?

Coral: Watching history repeat itself, love. Watching history repeat itself.

Anonymous

I wrote this entry at the beginning of the Gulf War and the beginning of my own journey of re-membering/reliving sexual assaults I underwent as a child.

The other day I turned on the news and the US army was in Saudi Arabia in a huddle with "cocked" raised rifles in one hand and holding (and "cocking") their penises with the other — chanting, like they do in huddles at a football game. I just sat there numb. My theory that penises and cannons, rifles, guns, etc., ... are one and the same was reinforced. My theory that guns are fabricated in the images of erect penises and the bullets were unwanted semen — shifted from theory to reality (i.e., rape). I cannot help viewing penises as another tool, a military tool that is used daily on women around the world.

And as the so-called Patriots declare war on Iraq (so that Iraq will "pull out"), they fire these "semen" at each other. Similarly men declare war on women daily as they use their penises as a weapon to control and terrorize us women. My happy thought for the day!

Bad Girl Liar

This was my first Women's Studies journal entry after returning to the education system after a decade in the work force. I was surprised and delighted that Women's Studies exists.

The article about naming and women "The Naming of Women" by Sheila Ruth struck me most profoundly. I notice it was also the most "masculine" in structure. At first I got excited. This is great. This is articulate, logical, non-blaming — I could come and show this to my father and he would understand what I keep trying to tell him about.

Then I got mad. Rage, seething, boiling, clench-my-jaw-and fists, find-something-and-smash-it mad. Then I looked over my shoulder (even though I was home alone). Because I do not doubt that this is a dangerous article — and that seeing the issues plainly and speaking up about them is a dangerous thing — so I pushed that anger back down inside — and felt the familiar rising wave of helplessness. Yes, I see it. The step-by-step, systematic undermining of females. Yes, I live in it and it hurts. I want to make that hurt go away. The anger is always there. It's a stupid, senseless, vitality-robbing system for both sides, men and women. Why can't more of us see that and change it? I have been sexually, physically and emotionally abused by men in my family and by my mother. She pushed me down harder than any of the men. For thinking? For asking screamingly obvious questions. So now I have phrases to describe her P.O.V. She is a masculine-identified woman ... but you know what? That doesn't shift the hurt — or the rage, or the fear. The constant editing and watching my back because my God Damn personality seeks to be acknowledged. I could scream.

Elaine Dornan

How do we challenge the assumptions and words of ourselves and others without implying that we or they are not okay?

Ageism, sexism, racism, classism, homophobia and all the other -isms and phobias I haven't named. Are they not all part of the problem? Shouldn't we speak up whenever someone says, "Well, it's not that I have anything against them — but ..."

I hear these kind of words being spoken in Women's Studies and again, in the hallway, afterwards. This time the target is older people. A woman tells us how her grandfather says he figures the world will be a better place when all his generation has died off. After class, another woman tells me that she figures nothing will change until all the "old boys" are dead and gone because they are all too old, too slow and too entrenched to change. When I ask how many older people she knows she tells me, "None, really." After all she doesn't go to bingo or have anything in common with older people. I tell her I know lots of older people who are incredible: burning with life, radical thinkers, militant environmental and political activists, quiet feminists, noisy feminists, sweet old women and men with gentle souls, some not so sweet or gentle but every one of them with a story to tell. The woman I am speaking with thinks the older people I am talking about must be the exception, and the ones she doesn't know, the rule.

I feel guilty writing this. This isn't about judging, but it feels like it. It's hard to be critical of words and attitudes without feeling like you're criticizing the people speaking the words. But I'm not. I know we all are indoctrinated into this ageist, racist, sexist culture; it makes my soul weep and I need the tools to fight back.

Pearl Kirby

I wanted to talk about a conversation I had with a young man I know. He asked me what I thought of this non-sexist spelling — "nonsense." He asked me what I thought of it and did the other women in my class "agree" with it. He felt that our English language is just fine, and why should we change it?

He was specifically complaining about the spelling of WOMAN. He said that if it's spelled "womyn" or "womiin," then we're rejecting the word "man," and "men" as well. What can you say to something like that? I explained to him that words — specifically nouns — were made to describe things as accurately as possible. The word "woman" doesn't describe us accurately at all. The "woman" implies that there is something male about me. As far as I know there is nothing masculine about me. Therefore, the word "woman" is not accurate in describing me.

I gave him an example, I said, "How would you feel if I called you a blond-brunette, or other people black-brunettes or red-brunettes?" That would be silly, but that's what happens when we use the words "female," "woman," "person," "history," etc. He agrees with what I was saying, but unfortunately I didn't get a reply from him. Smoke was coming out of the back of my car and we got distracted and never finished the conversation.

Gina Marina Cifuentes Faena

New thoughts, old stories. Mama always talking about caterpillars, hates them hmmnn. I reflect how it was her stage of life when she was a caterpillar, not happy, not rewarding. Sure, immigrant women, no language skills, told to "LEARN ENGLISH. You're in Canada now." She submits, takes away her easy tongue movements and tries to twist her lips and tongue to conform to english. But she got lost in this language. Maybe she had so many things she tried to tell me, but her language waited to tell me. Not this FUCKING language. This language created a strange gap.

My vice-principal spoke to me one day while I was walking through the empty desolate cafeteria when I was nine or ten years old. Mr. Skinner who wasn't skinny, he was this fat, balding-hair-combed-to-cover-up-his-balding head-man, said, "Gina." "Yes," I answer. "Your mother doesn't speak english." I wanted to scream in his face tell him, "Yes, she does. I understand her. We talk. I don't speak spanish, but, yes, we talk. Why do you tell me? There is no meaning to your statement? Do YOU speak spanish? WHY DO YOU SAY THIS, to make me feel as empty as this lunchroom, to hate my mother because she is different? WHY!" She nursed me, she changed me, she remembers playing with her sisters and I am part of that memory she sees me with her. Please don't take that away. But you do, you did.

Crying now. Funny I speak fluent spanish now. Now is too late. It is not our way, we both struggle in english, we converse in english. We have gotten lost in english. So many events these past weeks, personal, yucky personal how do I get through it, Machete in hand trying to cut a path. For some reason I come to school, get a warm honey almond milk, and in its comfort stand up in the jungle and move forward. It's like a feeling of cuddle bug, a warm snug hug, a suckle from my mama's breast a kiss and a gentle push to go on.

Chapter Four

BRINGING IT
HOME

Chapter Four

BRINGING IT HOME

IN THIS CHAPTER, there is a wide assortment of topics, many of which are found in earlier chapters and sections. This chapter compiles examples of women integrating new learning with their daily experience — how they 'bring it home'.

The contributors take new concepts and theories from classroom discussions and course material to use in understanding and coping with their world. Many of the women describe changes in their perspective and in their activism. One writer describes how she has found support for her ideas on non-sexist childrearing, allowing her to make changes with her sons about housework and to "never hit girls." Another woman explains that her work in the pro-choice movement is to "counter-balance" her father's involvement in a right-to-life group.

The entries take us into these women's lives: to their activities in the home, to their workplaces, to marches and demonstrations, to their schools, and to their everyday existence. We get to see some of the ways these women experience these episodes and events with the added dimension of feminist consciousness filtered through their individual personalities.

Each piece in this chapter takes a wide view: looking at the roots of power imbalances, past the basic comprehension of inequities and towards social change — asking the question, what can I do about it? This chapter is about feminist movement that takes place on all levels and at all times in our new learning. In fact, journal writing itself assists social change. When our thoughts are spoken or recorded, they become part of the revolution. Writing it down is powerful and dangerous.

— DANA

Gunnel Susanne Tesfa

This was my second entry in my first Women's Studies course. My first entry was formal and stiff, because that is usually the requirement in school, but my instructor's reassuring response to the first entry showed me that it was safe to follow my feelings when writing, which I did in this entry.

I thought I knew about women's oppression
I thought I knew about inequality
I thought I knew about unfair treatment
I thought I knew about the voice
     that does not speak up.
I thought I knew all about it because
     I am a woman.
I thought nobody can tell me about my role and status
in society.
I thought all I can learn are some names and data
about heroines of the women's movement,
some numbers and digits about events
     that took place.

But I learn, slowly and surprisingly, that I am denying
women's oppression inequality unfair treatment.
I learn that I do not really believe with all my heart
that we are oppressed disadvantaged disregarded.
I learn that I don't dare to believe it because it is
an uncomfortable truth, a truth that weakly shines
     through my closed eyes,
a truth I cannot ignore any longer.

I start to shake off the guilt and the shame I feel
about this truth,
I don't want to feel discouraged — I want to feel
strong.
I can feel how frightened I am to let go of the belief
that the men's values, knowledge, and ways of thinking
are the only valid ones.
But my resistance is growing with the acceptance

of the wisdom and the strength of women.
It is scaring to feel the protecting blanket sliding
down, but it is liberating at the same time.

Elaine Dornan

I'm not as tired anymore. The fight is as hard and complex as ever.
And I still dare to dream.

This is my fourth term at Langara; at first, I was so overwhelmingly grateful to be in college I absorbed without much critical evaluation. Last term I learnt the danger of this, so now I listen and analyze carefully. For me an education is a way out of poverty, and the beginnings of independence. Yet many of the courses feel like exercises in mental wizardry, with the instructors showing off their great intellect to dazzle and impress us (or maybe to impress themselves) but never to delve into the meat of the discipline (after all, if we learn the sorcerers' tricks ...). I see Women's Studies as an alternative, a place where I can have control, where, if I choose, I can challenge my assumptions, beliefs and values, and define my own knowledge base.

Sitting in Women's Studies last night, talking about how women are represented in advertising, I became confused. I understood advertising as a powerful knowledge system but I'd forgotten about it. Making decisions about what shoes, clothes or food to buy based on what other people wear and advertisements has not been, nor is, my reality. Trying to figure out how to feed, clothe and provide transportation for three children and one adult on approximately $200 per month has been my reality.

Most of the women I know are single mothers and in similar financial situations, and our only criteria for buying is necessity and if it's second-hand or free. Many of us live with our poverty in denial and affect political righteousness. I deny I lost my son to poverty; I didn't encourage him to leave home the day after he graduated because it costs less to feed three than four but because of his great job offer up north. I tell myself that my children and I don't want new clothes (I'm reusing, recycling and reducing), that TV brainwashes us and we don't have desserts because white sugar has no place in our bodies. I tell myself that the strongest political statement I can make is the way I spend my money and I will not give this system my money. But there really isn't any money to give.

In other times I've had good-paying jobs and substantial savings accounts. All this changed in 1982 when my daughter was born with a birth defect and I started spending my life in specialists' offices and hospitals. By the time she was four I was diagnosed as having cancer, and endometriosis, and told I was pregnant again. I was told I should consider an abortion followed by a hysterectomy. Two years after the baby was born I finally gave in to that hysterectomy; it saved my life but at a very high price. As a single parent living on welfare (my partner left because he couldn't cope with my illness), I felt weak, trapped and had no self-esteem. As my physical strength returned I started putting the pieces back together again.

I learnt to drive, got a car, moved to subsidized housing and went back to school (I had dropped out in grade eight). My son and two daughters helped and encouraged me and, with a lot of luck, I succeeded in all these goals. Accomplishing these goals allowed me to dare to dream again; clarifying my focus and drive, consolidating my organizational and perseverance skills helped me attempt college. So now I'm in college and on a student loan, which is okay, there's a bit of extra money, but my self-esteem is still low. And I'm tired all the time, tired of fighting for my mental and physical well-being.

I really don't know why this stuff came to the surface in Women's Studies last night but perhaps, for the first time, I looked at myself and realized I don't want to live in denial anymore. In order to survive I've told myself everything's okay: I'm strong and can deal with the way many people pity me when they find out I am a single-parent and therefore, in their minds, a failure and someone who is dangerous to trust. I am strong and I will do whatever I have to and make it work. Then, when I heard the class talking about advertising denigrating and dehumanizing women and poverty I realized that my kids read and see those advertisements. I wondered if they judged themselves and me by ad standards. I wondered why my self-esteem was still so low. Because I've bought into the system more than I care to admit? Or is it because I finally faced the precariousness of every woman's position in this society and it scares the hell out of me? And because I am starting to understand what a hard and complex fight it will be.

Darcian Welychenko

Last night we saw [the NFB film] *Not a Love Story* as research for our group project. Watching was all right. Walking to my car after, I was very disturbed. The images wouldn't leave my head. The scenes of torture were like the ones I read about in Latin America. I read about the torture and couldn't picture it and then I saw it on the TV. That stuff isn't pretend. It happens every day under right-wing governments and is filmed for the voyeuristic pleasure of god knows who. Who watches that? Who would find pleasure in watching someone else's pain? What is it about our society that thrives on the glory of destruction and pain? I really hate it. I'm even like that.

As a child we all used to read about Nazis and talk about what they did. My parents and I went to a Jewish museum in Winnipeg and I remember staring at this bar of soap. I tried to imagine bathing with it. I was about eight and the museum or whatever was in the basement of a synagogue in the north end. You had to go in through this small door into this low-ceilinged room that was filled with pictures and horrible objects. Somehow the soap was worse than anything else. Had my great-grandparents stayed in Europe, what would have happened to them? Would bits of what would become me be in that soap? No one is too far removed not to be a part of every lampshade, of every blanket infested with smallpox, of every image of a woman in pain.

I keep thinking that, had I not been raised in a perfect little working-middle-class home, where would I be? Had the stars moved, had the fates blinked, could I not be in a brothel in Thailand right now, might I not be locked up in some east-side apartment with my torture and pain being filmed for someone else's pleasure? Even though I am here, even though I am safe and healthy, is there someone projecting these images onto me? How many men on the street don't see me as I am, but rather imagine me bound and gagged.

Bonnie

Coming from a culture that believes a woman's only role is to be a good wife.

Taking a Women's Studies course had been a great experience for me. I always had a limited space and accepted it. Now I feel different. I am more confident and can take control.

I can speak to other women about not allowing themselves to be treated differently because of their gender.

I am even educating my sons that women have a special place in the world and that they should always be treated with respect. My sons do not always agree, but they do have an open mind and do their share of housework.

I think this is neat because for a while they thought it was a woman's job. Another thing I teach them is never hit girls.

Elaine Dornan

Although schools function to maintain and perpetuate the inequalities of our society, subversive actions can and do take place in schools.

Every day I come across ideas and actions that cause me to reflect upon the changing landscape of my mind and the world I inhabit. A couple of days ago, when I was at my daughter's school, an incident happened I would like to share. One of the boys in [my daughter's] grade-five class was exhibiting racist and sexist behaviour. He called a girl in her class an extremely racist name and tried to get the other kids to agree that she should be excluded from the chess tournament. The girls in the class told him he was racist and sexist and they wouldn't put up with it. They said he knew the girls were going to "whip his ass at chess and because he was so sexist he couldn't take it." They then informed him that racist and sexist thinking was fucked and if he wanted anyone to stay in one piece he better figure it out. The boys in class listened to this, and after the girls were finished, reinforced what they said by telling him that they thought he was a jerk too.

It was great hearing those girls tell that boy the problem was his, I was surprised and happy, but at the same time anxious. So I suggested they go tell the teacher. My daughter wanted to know why, "since we are perfectly capable of handling this ourselves." Although I was pleased and proud, I also felt uneasy. Upon reflection I realized my anxiety stemmed from the norm of females not displaying anger. These girls were mad and vocal and in his face, and it worried me; somehow I felt like big brother was going to swoop down and censor them. That they would be seen as bitches, shrews and nags. That their mothers weren't raising them "properly." I never realized how much I'd bought into this particular little trap before.

Gloria E. Roque

As a woman of colour in Canada, I am still in the process of appropriating and defining my feminity. There have been no positive changes in the Immigration Act regarding the concerns of domestic workers.

When doing all my research for my optional project, in which I chose to interview some women at the Philippine women's centre about domestic workers, I came upon an article which dealt with women and femininity and the differences of the roles between white women and women of colour. It is a fascinating article. I am still trying to digest it. It deals with society's dominant ideology in which the ideal role for a white woman emphasizes domesticity and motherhood, and for women of colour this ideology and institutions have had no problem accepting women of colour as workers first and foremost, even when this worker status is achieved at the expense of separating women from their families and children.

For many women of colour, domesticity and motherhood have been constructed through their employment as domestics and surrogate mothers to white families rather than in relation to their own families. After reading Sedef Arat-Koc's article "In the Privacy of Our Own Home ..." I decided to look for more articles and found this one entitled "Immigration Policies, Migrant Domestic Workers and Definition of Citizenship in Canada" — what an amazing essay! The fact that domestic workers can't bring their children and families to Canada until they have their landed-immigrant status and can prove financial stability to qualify as sponsors just emphasizes this separation. I interviewed a woman at the centre and she hasn't seen her children for six years. She is desperately trying to prove financial stability, but it is hard when your pay is low and you have to send money home too!

Lidwina Bautista

Although I have been in Canada for over twenty years, I was born and raised in the Philippines. I was driving along Cambie Street one day and saw a Filipina nanny walk by. She inspired me to write this poem.

THE CYCLE CONTINUES

I see her — a small, brown woman pushing
a baby carriage behind a white woman;
    sadness envelopes my heart, weep I say
    will my weeping free her or console her?
I see their passive faces
wanting to disappear and hide their faces
educated women, forced to flee the
poverty and bleak future at home.

I wonder what she is thinking
fear of people laughing and feeling sorry for her
JUST A NANNY, a maid, must comply to
her master's wishes/commands or
be sent back to her past from which
she is trying to run away

Hush, hush
Silence
Yes, Ma'am Yes, Sir
Anything I can do for you?

My children ask me.
"Mom, why do you call Philippines home?
You live here, Canada is your home."
I wonder why ...

In my silence, a stranger asked
"Where did you come from?"
Colour immigrants, trying to survive
"Go back to your own country,
you're stealing our jobs."

History speaks loudly
head tax on Chinese
internment camps for Japanese
Let's keep Canada white

I see the future
My children all grown-up
born and raised in Canada
A stranger asks them
"Where did you come from?"

Varney Allis

Sometimes I found that Women's Studies helped me to understand current events in my life that otherwise might have left me floundering and feeling utterly hopeless.

I've been reading the readings too, and think of it all as a background to my life. What I realize now from taking this course, is that as events happen in my life, I can see them reflected back at me in a different way, reflected out of the context of all our readings and discussions.

Some things have happened these two weeks — some a reflection of patterns in my family life, and some are new and unprecedented and tragic. The main change is that someone who is important to my eight year-old-son committed suicide. She is also important to me too, and I must say, as I feel through the sadness, that this still remains out of my grasp. I can't understand it and I can't believe it. She was the out-of-school supervisor of [my son's] program. He'd spend his afternoons with her and two other staff from 3:00 pm to 6:00 pm. She was (can I really use the past tense) someone who really understood kids.

Certainly she was different from many of us parents — we seemed more middle-class and heterosexual in contrast — but that difference was something positive for me — a woman who described herself as "androgyny personified," who had energy and a mischievous streak that came out as humour in the face of the typical chaos of the day. I had hired her too, doing the interview with another parent and staff person. This put me in the position of being one of her main contact people — for parents and for issues concerning the running of the centre. I used to talk to her a lot.

One thing that bothers me (aside from how my son is really dealing with it — he cries when he goes to sleep sometimes now) is that she seemed to have survived a difficult childhood by being able to analyze what had happened to her. She had completed a university degree in Political Science and Women's Studies. She was a radical feminist in every way. She didn't survive in the end — why? And what does this mean? Is this the most awful consequence that someone who speaks their heart's truth faces?

I have my own pain/sadness/despair/void that I sometimes glimpse and suffer over. That in itself is about as much of that kind of pain that I can bear. And yet I am sure this is not the depths of her pain — as I think of conversations with her, and how she sometimes said she'd been crying that day — how much was she talking about a pain that I can't even imagine, let alone feel? I think of a great gap between us that I didn't even know was there, until now. A gap in understanding — a gap caused by my words spoken and heard, but a different meaning received. It's as if we were speaking different languages without knowing.

My question then — how to regain control and keep my sanity when crises invade all parts of me, even the parts that I keep tightly protected (that protected part is me writing). So what I'm saying is that these crises even steal my stolen time.

Jackie Lynne

I don't know ...

FRAGMENTS

A fragment
To my surface
Floats,
Jagged,

A shard that cuts,
And jars my consciousness.

Hangs suspended.

A frozen frame
Out of time.
Displaced.
A thin shred of horror.
Sharp.
Stark
Under my senses' gaze.

From its edges,
Blood drops
Cold.
Fills my eyes,
my hands,
Floods my heart with
Searing pains.

Echoes in my ears,
A heartbeat,
Remember?
In my throat ...
A scream,
Centuries long,
Womb-loud
Roars me 'round
and 'round
The World.

And ...

Drops me on
the outermost edges of my breath.

I stand.
A lighthouse
Watching.

A fragment
To my surface
Floats,
Jagged.

Tracey Herbert

*Reading this entry reminds me of how being perceptive and aware
of what is happening around you can make you feel really alone
even when you're in a ballroom with two or three hundred people.*

This suicide conference is a joke. Upper-class balding men intellec-
tualizing about suicide patterns, degrees of lethality. How to mea-
sure this and that.

A woman challenges an analogy that compares suicide's lack of
funding and AIDS overfunding as per death rate. The man tells her

she doesn't understand as he waves his hand repeatedly in her direction, "you don't understand the analogy."

These people never touch on the subject of society, of patriarchy as the oppressor, responsible for the majority of dysfunction of the people in this world.

They bash away at the government people and politicians, blaming them for lack of concern. No shit. How can they acknowledge Canadian society sucks, it's failing.

Compared to the average Canadian suicide rate, native peoples are killing themselves the most. Maybe they (white experts) just use the graphs to show how normal they are.

Suicide is still prevalent among non-natives.

The conference is a power-over situation — Time limits. Be quiet. Ask appropriate questions. It stresses me out to be here.

Oh well, there is some new info, but I think everybody missed the boat. I also noticed all the non-native people sat in front and the native people sat at the very back and sides.

I sat in the middle. Is that because I am a 1/2 breed?

B. J.

It was scary breaking my anonymity. I was afraid of being rejected, but it was more important to me to write honestly and openly about what was really going on.

This weekend has brought me a lot of hope. Attending the Vision for Women Alcoholics Anonymous conference broke through many blocked emotions for me. I was extremely moved by what I heard, the tremendous courage these women have and the miracle of their sobriety. I was really encouraged by the many feminist view points I heard expressed and was particularly validated and relieved to attend the workshop entitled "Feminists in AA: Don't let the language send you out!" I feel there are many women who are extremely angry about issues that go well beyond language, and that many of them are working for change within the structure of the program.

This experience has given me encouragement to not simply write the program off and all of its positive aspects. The whole feel of the conference fit my feminist being. For once I didn't feel I had to separate my feminist side from my recovery which has been a very big problem for me and as I heard this weekend, for many women in the program. For the time being, I am feeling that once again I can receive the support I so wish to have and yet not suffocate my feminism in order to receive that support. I truly believe that my personal recovery needs my feminism and that my feminism needs the work I do on myself in recovery. Gloria Steinem talks at length about this in her book *Revolution from Within: A Book of Self-Esteem.* The farther I go in this journey the more this makes sense to me.

Michelle Cannon-Burley

My decision to do my journal on abortion was an easy one. Abortion has always been a part of my life in some way. As a child I was bombarded with it being wrong to kill an unborn child.

My father was the president of the Right-to-Life Association (very active Pro-Life Roman Catholic). As the youngest of twelve children and a girl, I wasn't allowed to speak, and when I did speak it wasn't heard. I always believed that only the person in any given circumstance could know what was best for them. And I learned very young not to believe everything I was told, after being sexually abused at ages five to six, nine to eleven, and sixteen to nineteen by a couple of my brothers, while being told sex was wrong and life was precious. When there was so much killing in the world over silly things, and seeing how unrespected children were treated I came to the conclusion my father was not speaking out of everyone's reality.

Since leaving home, I now have started having a voice and I've also been able to learn more about an issue which affects all women to some degree, if they have chosen to not have children at different times in their lives and been faced with thinking that they might be pregnant. The thought must cross their minds. I know it did mine at least once.

I see firsthand what happens to women and children of births that weren't wanted, and I don't believe that it has to be this way, nor should it be this way. I often wonder how my father could say he was a right-to-lifer and be a Civil Libertarian. They are rather contradictory in my opinion, since making someone have a child they don't want, can't afford or can't psychologically care for tends to take away from that women's civil rights and liberties.

I guess my idea of getting involved actively and doing things like journals and report papers on abortion is that I am counter-balancing the involvement of the rest of my siblings and parents in the anti-abortion process.

Pati Mathias

Dr. Garson Romalis was shot the day I reread this piece and I could not help but compare the style of protest chosen by the UBC students to that which I feel is protest taken to a repulsive extreme.

I was driving to Langara to work on an assignment last weekend and had occasion to cross Granville at 16th Avenue. The entire intersection was surrounded by a "UBC STUDENTS AGAINST ABORTION" demonstration. The traffic light was red and as I sat waiting *I* began to see red. The group was exclusively *young* people who all held signs that read "ABORTION KILLS BABIES." They waved their signs at me and the other traffic as we passed them. I was enraged; then embarrassed and confused by my reaction.

I later began to think clearly and to compare this gathering to the pro-abortion rally that I attended this fall in front of Kim Campbell's office. My first thought was that I should not begrudge these students the expression of their point of view. One of the over-whelming feelings I had at the pro-choice rally was an appreciation at being able to express ourselves on what has become such a very political matter. I begrudged those young women and men that right, though, because I questioned their motives. I am not con-vinced that they see beyond the inflammatory slogan. As surely as abortion kills "babies," illegal abortion kills women along with those "babies." Not having the right to reproductive determination is cen-tral to all of this.

If only a fraction of the resources, funding and energy that go into such senseless pursuits as the cure to male baldness, exploration of outer space, and war, war, war went into creating safe and cultural-ly acceptable (women's cultures) birth control methods, we *would* have alternatives to "killing our babies." I have been party to a num-ber of damaging and unsuccessful forms of birth control myself. One day, in my twentieth year, I went to have my birth control pill (C-Quens) prescription refilled and was told that they were no longer available because they were dangerous to health. No one suggested that there might be a health risk to me when I started to take them three years before. Right now I am involved in a class-action suit against the manufacturer of the Dalkon Shield. The use of it injured me, but I will never know the extent of the damage done, as I have never attempted to become pregnant. More than once I have listened to and comforted my friends as they agonized about their abortions.

I see that all these methods of dealing with choice are choices in themselves. They are not very good choices and I can't help but feel that my rage at the anti-abortion activists is tied up with these com-plexities. Despite the complexity, I still single out one issue, that of being able to choose to abort or not to abort without question, qualification, condition or judgement. I saw red because I feel that the anti-abortion protesters stand in the way of *every* woman's right to choose privacy and safety.

Karen Egger

Now working full-time, still much the same dilemma exists for me. I feel my energies are drained by the demands of my job and I have little time or energy remaining for other activities in my life.

Having completed this week's readings for both my Women's Studies courses, my mind is whirling and working away, creating new thoughts, concepts, ideas out of the old information and the new. And lots of questions. My current major awareness, and dilemma, is what I'd like to explore a little, not even sure exactly what form it takes, just some of its components. I have been becoming slowly, reluctantly, convinced that action is necessary to change the way things are and that I have a responsibility to facilitate or take part in some of that action, and that I'm very reluctant to do so. I see myself, although oppressed, also as an oppressor, and as a part of a privileged group, reluctant to give up some of any privilege.

These are very uncomfortable realizations. I keep on trying to deny them, excuse myself, and at the same time feel dissatisfied, unsettled about what I'm doing in an uncertain kind of manner. I am becoming painfully aware (trying not to on some level, though) that I'm very privileged to be participating in this patriarchal model of learning, however reluctantly so. It's as if I'm walking forward, finding a path for myself, acting, but finding that the way is full of questions, uncertainties, dilemmas, paradoxes, complexities. Following a path of learning because it is a safer world for me to be in than one of direct action. Acting on what I know and understand right now.

It's not true that direct action is something I shy away from; it's a question more of time. And that ties into privilege, and how I choose to spend my time. By spending the time to get good marks, learn something, I have little time left over to devote to actions to improve, to facilitate change. I am feeling guilty I suppose (a way to avoid responsibility for my actions?). Why am I in school? Because I saw that as a better option than getting a job. Why? 'Cause I didn't think I could get a job that would pay decently and I'd enjoy, find meaningful. And I wanted to take Women's Studies.

Now that I'm in there in this removed, abstracted, intellectual world, I want to act, but don't have the time to. Feel guilty when I see people who are acting who have very little time, or when I am asked to participate in something, or when I take some time out to do something I really enjoy.

Conflicted! But it has been good to write about, to get some of those jumbled emotions and thoughts out. Know that I fear acting in some ways because I fear getting caught up, consumed, being unable to define my limits and boundaries.

Tracey Herbert

The ranch in this entry is a symbol of the land I have always desired for myself and my displaced family.

Last night I dreamt I quit my job and became a writer. I went home to my grandparents and recorded the complete history of our family and the elders in our communities.

Of course, I became famous. In the book I started a Native University which focused on Indian history and culture. Ranching and rodeoing were also a big part of the plan. We would raise cattle, good horses and be self-sufficient.

Michael Jackson read my book and came up to visit my family. He gave me the money I needed ($20 million) and I put the ranch in my grandparents' name.

Of course, I ran the school and imposed my beliefs on everyone, as if I were God.

Then I dreamt about Brian Mulroney. He threatened me because my book outlined a new set of laws for Indians and he said I had no right to change the laws. We argued and I forget the rest.

This has been a very emotional week for me. The report I did restimulated a lot of old hurts. I love my family very much, and to really understand how badly they were discriminated against is almost too hurtful.

Gloria E. Roque

This was my first woman's march. As I look back to that night, I am still amazed at the power we women have when we get together. I am still caught in the Catch-22, though.

I went to the "Take back the Night" rally on September 24. It was just incredible. This was the first women's march I have ever gone to. I am very active politically but this was the first time that I had been together with about 2,000 women. It was amazing, the energy indescribable. I cried during most of the speakers as it made me feel so emotional that there were all these women that had gathered on that Friday night for a cause they believed in: To take back the Night. And we did succeed. It does make me angry that we have to be extra-careful when going out alone. It just isn't fair. I went with my two closest female friends and we shared a wonderful experience together.

But I have been in a Catch-22 about the issues of "Tokenism" — the majority of the speakers at the rally were women of colour. That felt good, but at the same time I wondered why, since we, as women of colour, are not the majority in the established women's groups. Yes, there are a lot of women-of-colour groups, but unfortunately we are quite marginalized from the mainstream movement. It's sad but true — obviously we must change this, because after all we are all sisters, but at the same time how will we do it? Our visibility can work for or against us in political issues. So I kick myself for thinking this because it did look and feel great to see women of colour appropriating our own voice and speaking out.

Michelle Elizabeth Neilson

I think I thought that the problem of jerky male supervisors on the job would somehow go away one day. Unfortunately, they're still around.

The class is really benefiting me; the readings are very hard-core, but it's the first time in college that I'm not falling asleep when studying.

I think Women's Studies is something I want to continue with. I think it's largely because of this course, the empowerment that I am feeling gradually, that helped me to handle a male superior's "out of line" behaviour at work. Even though I was new on the job and didn't know him very well, I refused to let a racist joke he told one day go unnoticed. After that he slapped my behind "playfully" one day in front of my immediate male supervisor. I was angry, and instead of playing along (which at one time I would have done) I assertively told him never to touch me again, ever. I realize I could have filed a complaint right there, but I decided I would prefer to warn the pathetic, uneducated, immature, power-tripping, female-phobic slob and if he tried anything again I would report it to whatever organization. I thought about how many women endure this kind of treatment and much worse, never speaking up, because they're afraid, afraid no one will believe them, afraid of losing their jobs. I was angry and well within my rights to call my boss on racism and sexism. Since then his attitude (at least with me) has changed considerably. He has displayed remorse and possibly real humility. But unfortunately it's probably just because he's still a loser ... and just wants to get into my pants.

Bonnie

As a First Nations woman who has experienced all forms of abuse.

I do not usually feel safe in large groups, but I lived through this one. The Women's Studies courses have been great for me because I have truly changed as a person. I see myself as being so special to be a woman. My family seem to appreciate me more. They definitely respect me more. However, it really saddens my heart that there are so many others like me that will see no change. All I can do is be an example. I am going home to work for my community in the near future. I am still in the process of applying, although I was verbally accepted. I am so scared, but also excited. Wish me luck.

Chapter Five

AFTERWORDS

Chapter Five

AFTERWORDS

IN JUNE 1994, we convened two meetings to discuss journal writing with the contributors. Twenty women participated by attending one of these taped sessions or giving us their written responses to a set of questions. This chapter is based on the transcripts from the meetings and the written submissions.

We began by discussing the diaries and journals that women had written before taking Women's Studies. As discussed in the Introduction, these had taken a variety of forms, from the little plastic ones with broken locks to letters to best friends. They were private spaces in which they could record the events of daily life and try to sort out problems. However, even writing in their diaries was not always safe. Several women spoke about the violation, when brothers or sisters, mothers or lovers, or even landlords, read their journals without permission.

Elaine commented that she had never written any diaries or any journals:

> I grew up in a very abusive background and I couldn't have written about that. I would have been too terrified to write that down; it would have made it too real. When I started doing journal writing in Women's Studies, it took me a long time, but I really like the process, and I do it a lot now.

We then asked what they thought of writing journals as part of Women's Studies.

LAURIE: When I learned that journal writing was going to be a part of the required assignments, I was shocked. Something that I have done most of my life was now going to be recognized in the great halls of higher education. Frankly, it tickled me to think that my work would include assignments that are a joy to engage in. Education had never before demonstrated that kind of appeal.

MARGARET: Writing a journal that I knew someone else was going to see was really different and a much better experience. I really enjoyed taking the trouble to say what I really meant. The process of figuring out how to say it also helped me to understand what I meant.

LEAH MINUK: For me, journals are often just feeling things and I go back and read them and I go, "This makes no sense." [In the Women's Studies journals] you have to be analytical to a degree. So it gives it much more form — makes it much more solid.

PATTY: *Was it useful to your own learning process? Did it help clarify emotions and thoughts? Did it help integrate things? Was it a useful part of the course? And, if so, how? And, if not, how not?*

DARCIAN: I think it was useful because it got us to write. I wouldn't have written a journal if it wasn't for the class.

LEAH MINUK: I think it's wonderful to have a space where you can write. You don't have to worry if you're articulate or if your grammar's correct. For me that's a real release, right? 'Cause then I can really deal with the issue and not get all caught up in the form and the format and the editing. And you're also dealing with emotions in Women's Studies in a way that you don't any other place. So to be able to write them down without worrying about whether you're gonna get an A or a C ... makes it really safe and more worth doing to me.

VARNEY: Yeah, I got the impression that the main point of the journal writing was the process, that it didn't matter what you wrote about or how you wrote. And that was a really important thing, sort of an unlocking of one's fears, or blocks that you might have had about writing. Just glancing at my entries again, I think it did provide a very strong mode of self-reflection. I think the journal was a very important moment to bring the readings into relevance and make me really see what was going on. I think it actually caused a transformation.

GLORIA ELVIRA: Once you put something to writing, I feel something has to be done. I have to think about it. I have to work at it.

LAURIE: It encouraged me to become more questioning. It also served as a sounding board between what I was learning and what I was thinking. There was a lot of confusion for me in this time of life. Coming into a feminist consciousness was unsettling and met with a lot of internal resistance (really denial) and so the journal entries were my sanctuary.

KAREN: It helped me to integrate and to process what I was learning, the theory I was learning in the class with my own life and to draw relationships, to connect my personal experience with what we were learning. A place to explore that. It was usually very immediate too.

LAURA: It was very valuable. It captured ideas I had at the time I had them. Ideas that I probably would have dismissed and forgotten otherwise. Later they were there to build on. They also served as a focus of what was really important, what I wanted to follow up on in other contexts, such as other classes, or politically, etc.

STACY: In the Women and Social Change course, we had to choose a topic and then work on that topic for every entry of the journal. So, when it came time to do the next entry, you knew that you couldn't be at that same place that you were the week before. You had to somehow forge through it and for me I chose my relationship with my father, and it was just amazing. Really having to push, and having to try to find things to make things better, and then even better, and so, yeah, this is social change within a journal.

JOANNA: I was rereading what I wrote, thinking back on handing them in and getting them back — certainly total excitement, and very much pressing the edge. And so I just want to say I feel embarrassed — I feel a bit sheepish [seeing that I was] just trying to name things, trying to recognize them, trying to realize that it's not just personal, individual, something wrong with me, that's producing this experience in my life, but that it's attached to other things. I can see that when I look back on it. So, I don't think that I had any conscious kind of idea, like "This is what I'm learning in this," but I do know that some really important stuff occurred.

DEBBRA: For me, to be taking a Women's Studies class, and dealing with things, and then to be writing in the journal and speaking with somebody and have them not cut me down, or go, "What are you talking about? Where do you make these things up, Debbra?" I felt reassured and also reaffirmed, like I wasn't some kind of lunatic. I am making progress, my fears and my concerns were legitimate and they were valid.

Especially at that time in my life it really helped reaffirm who I was and helped me feel like, yeah, I'm on the right path and it's okay who I am, and I can stop making apologies or stop trying to scrunch myself into somebody else's mould. Because all my life there was always "You're clothes aren't fancy enough," or "You're not pretty enough" or "You're not skinny enough in the right places" or things like that. And so to finally have that space just to be me for who I was right then. I don't know, it was really exciting.

MARGARET: I want to follow up on something Leah said a little while ago. My first journal entry was not: "Am I crazy, but am I good? Am I smart? Do you understand what I am saying? Am I going to make it?" In the same way that, for Joanna, writing about her emotions was dangerous, it was very dangerous for me to write down what I think. Not just how do I feel about it, like it makes me happy or sad, but is this right? Is this not right?

So in and of itself, as an educational experience, it was completely valid, even without the rest of Women's Studies, although it's better if it's combined with the rest of Women's Studies. Particularly for an older student, such as myself, who has the life experience to be able to read the other elder writers, and go, "Yes, she's right! I've lived this, this is true." It was an ideal experience for me

ELAINE: When I first started I spent a lot of time worrying "Can I say this? Does this make any sense? Will it make any sense at all?" I can write academically. But I wanted to integrate academic writing with my personal voice, so that everything I write has my personal voice in it. Journal writing helped me do that. So now, when I write, it's not "Can I write this, am I allowed to say this?" it's "How can I say this the best? What words can I use to make this the clearest?" And I'm sure that the process of journal writing helped me to get to that spot.

DAPHNE: What I liked about it, yeah, you got marks for it [laughter]. I also liked the fact that the instructors got to know a part of me. I wasn't just some anonymous face in the classroom, which is really nice.

SIMA: Journal writing was a tool that helped me to organize my thoughts, my feelings, my emotions, my anger, my hatred and break up with a guy who — aaargh [laughter] ...

Sometimes I would have a problem in paper writing, and it really made me mad when I couldn't start and the due date is coming closer and closer. And then I would write and write and sometimes I would write my thesis statement in the journal: "Oh, that's it, I've got it." And then I start writing my paper, so it helped me that way, too. I could vent out my anger and feelings and whatever.

MARIA: I began when I was twenty. Women's Studies really helped me come into my own as a woman and as an adult. All of a sudden, everything you were learning up to that point was a total lie, and you feel so angry that society is giving you all these messages that are just bullshit, and in Women's Studies that feels so right, it's so emotional, so much comes up. It's not a course that you can just put your emotions on the shelf and just go ahead and do what the instructor wants. It's a course that changes your life.

It would be really hard not to have the journals — it's really hard to think analytically about something when you are going wild with every type of emotion, and it really helps to integrate learning. It's not just taking what the teacher says and spitting it back out — when it changes your life, and you break up with boyfriends and confront people, it overlaps with your whole life.

DANA: One of the important things about Women's Studies journals for me was that you got to say all those things that you didn't really get a chance to think of until after class. That's what makes it more concrete; you can confirm it by writing it down and thinking about it, and it doesn't end when the class ends.

PATTY: *What was it like having an instructor reading and responding to what you had written?*

VARNEY: I couldn't wait to read it. Knowing that it was going to be very positive, just commenting on things, or, "Why did you say that?". There was nothing negative. That was really important.

GLORIA ELVIRA: It was really neat to have the one-to-one with the instructor. You know you've had your time, even if you weren't able to speak in the class because it was so large.

PATTY: As an instructor, I felt it gave me a way to be in touch with what was going on for everyone in the room. It made it easier to figure out where to go next or what to do or where it was going or what worked or what didn't.

GUNNEL: At first I didn't know what it was going to be like, trying to edit everything that you are thinking. But then you give it to somebody, so basically you agree to trust this person. That was an amazing step. My very first entry sounds like I was restraining myself, so technical and without any depth. And then when I got it back, I felt whew [big sigh], "Oh, I see." [laughter] "So that's it! Okay." And then the next one was just the complete opposite of it, I just put everything in it. Having somebody actually read it, giving it in and getting it back and knowing that this person has really read it, was one of the most important things.

DAPHNE: Okay, sometimes the comments sounded too generic. There was this one entry that was really aggressively written and it was naming people, and then I got this really short comment, like "Good effort," but "I'm glad you found this outlet to express yourself." [laughter] What is this? What do you mean? Sometimes they seemed non-judgemental, which was good, and other times I was trying to get a reaction 'cause I was really mad about something, and then these comments that I had interpreted as non-judgemental were just too bland.

SIMA: The first time I received my journal back, I read my comment and I found out that everybody else had comments and I thought, "No, that's just impossible, teachers don't do that. I'm sure they hire someone to do it for them." [lots of laughter] And I wanted to see the comments, to see if the handwriting matched. How many people are reading them?

I was curious about this for the first month or so. I compared the handwriting. I just didn't believe it. And then I enjoyed it when I proved to myself, that's really the teacher, they really do it. So then I liked it very much.

CHRISTIE: At first I had lots of anxiety, but I found it incredibly helpful and that's part of what made it such a good learning tool — the encouragement, having someone who responds to what you write. Especially when I wrote some things in my journal that I wasn't talking about with the people in my life, writing from some secret place, and someone could respond without having to have a face-to-face interaction. I could put things out there and get some responses. It also increases your connection with the instructor in the course in ways that you don't necessarily otherwise get. Sometimes the response from the instructor allows you to see another side of the woman teaching the course that you don't see during class. You find you had a common experience that you might not otherwise find out about. That was really valuable to me. It was easier for me to learn with someone I connected with — she's real!

TERRY: I died for my responses. Each time so much hinged on it. Like the entry where I tunnelled so deep into my murk that I revealed secrets that I'd resolved to never air. The night this one was due back I ran face-to-face into my instructor. She reddened visibly after saying "Hi" and I fainted inside. I thought I'd said too much. She thought I was weird, sick. Maybe I was, but I couldn't afford to believe it: I had to survive.

This is the only conflict for me. For the most part, I believe journal writing is good. I don't believe it shaped my thoughts in any intrusive way. But I am concerned in retrospect. I was very fragile then, as I know others were as well. With our instructors not there to do therapy, if serious stuff gets triggered, we might find ourselves with nowhere to go. Sometimes the replies were much like a bandage, very gently and skillfully placed over the wounds I exposed. Sometimes they were mildly mirrored formula. I wondered how it felt to be the "instructor." Did they feel as paralyzed and inadequate as I felt sometimes?

DOROTHY: *There are instructors now writing about Women's Studies journals and about their negative experiences with them. One of the articles we've read [by Keith Louise Fulton] talks about some of this. She suggests that journals are no different from every other kind of exercise: basically they're to get women to think what the teacher wants them to think. What's your reaction to that?*

LAURIE: I think that students' thoughts are getting shaped with every instructor and this is part of the academic training to develop a sense of individual thought. Good instructors are the ones that help facilitate this with the student. Women's Studies challenged me and my belief system, yet never condemned it.

LEAH MINUK: I found my journal entries shaped a heck of a lot less than any of my other academic papers, because I never felt in journal writing in Women's Studies that I was performing and expected to come to a point of view. This is causing quite a rise in me. And yet every academic paper I have written, even within Women's Studies, there has always been that hand, because there is no such thing as "objective."

KATE: I think this is really interesting, because it's something that seems to be coming up in Women's Studies a lot — the issue of power differences between instructor and student and how we deal with that. It sometimes can become a problem. I really felt that the journals were definitely the one place where that didn't happen.

MARGARET: I felt that it was a contract between teacher and student. If it was okay for me to hand in as finely crafted a piece of work as I could possibly sweat out in two weeks, or something else that I wrote five minutes before the class started, that I was going to allow the instructor that same privilege. Maybe a lot of things happened and she didn't have enough time to write anything very good, or [else] she felt really inspired and she was able to give great feedback and good questions. And, perhaps I flatter myself, but I figure I have just as much of a chance of influencing the instructor as vice versa. So I didn't feel there was any coercion involved. I really felt it as a correspondence.

JOANNA: Yeah, I'm glad you said that, because when you were asking about shaping I thought a vigorous yes, yes, yes, shaped for sure. But what I notice is that, when I would start to get into despair, usually the response would be: "Yeah, its pretty bad isn't it, have you thought about this?" Either ask me to look at something, or ask me whether this makes a difference or not. In the Women and Social Change one, there was a particular instruction to write, to record the resistance. And that was a very interesting process for me because, in the beginning of that process, I could not distinguish resistance anywhere. I thought there was no history of resistance. So, I would say for sure, definitely and urgently, that there is [a need] to offer something. I mean isn't that what teachers are paid to do?

PATTY: That's part of my idea on it, the word I keep using a lot is that it is "messy." Journals are really messy, they are not a neat, easy, categorical part of the course. It is truly one of the places that we acknowledge our emotions, our bodies, our souls as [being as] important as our minds. And I do think that's not an easy thing to do in an academic setting. So there is a part of people backing off from it because of that, but I also think there is a part of people backing off because it is messy and it's hard to know what any of us should do once we're in there. You know, there isn't an easy answer.

KATE: I think what works about them is precisely that there is no standard; there is no standard of correctness for how this thing is supposed to turn out and, yeah, that is threatening, because when people do start to speak from their experience, instead of from the mould, it's powerful.

DEBBRA: For me, that was the one place that I felt the safest. I think part of it was knowing that it was my book; I brought it home, I could write in it wherever, and then I could hand it in, and I didn't have to see her face when she read it, and then I just safely got it back from the pile and then I could go off and read what she had to say.

KAREN: To me I think, so what if it shaped me? You know? It's an incredibly valuable tool. Like you said, it's far less shaped than any other thing you ever have a chance to put out, in academia.

DAPHNE: When you're writing in a journal for a course, for school, you don't really know where to draw the line, I guess. I really enjoyed it, and I liked it the most because it felt like the most unscholastic exercise to me. But I guess I'm fortunate because I've never had anything too devastating happen to me, so I never had anything get too personal, taking too big of a risk like that, and then getting judged or marked for it.

CHRISTIE: There's always going to be a limitation, because you are writing something to be handed in, which is different from writing something that you aren't going to give anyone permission to read. But that doesn't invalidate journal writing.

LAURA: I think any time we interact with anyone, it's possible and likely that they will in some ways change the configuration of our thoughts. I don't really see why it should be more of a threat in journal writing than in lectures, or in conversation. Of course if a person was being marked on what you actually put into your journal, it would certainly affect the degree to which you'd be willing to write honestly.

ELAINE: I find even when I write for myself, I censor myself. There's just some things that I just don't want to look at, or can't look at, or it just doesn't happen, it just sits there flat on the paper and I have nothing to say. Sometimes I'm just not willing to push it.

GUNNEL: What I found was there was the balance between the journal pushing me to think about things, and on the other hand, it being up to me about how much I want to say, and what I want to say.

SIMA: I felt this class gap, not only race but the class gap is so huge. I'm coming from a very poor, working-class background. So I think there might be things that people can't write about because they're so different from the whole dominant culture surrounding them. There are so many things that the middle class don't get, they just don't understand it. I guess it's not negative, it just doesn't reflect the total of me in that class. This is just a little, little bit of Sima, who's been at Langara in Vancouver.

The way to resolve the problem is not by saying, "Oh, it's negative and let's not do it"; the way to resolve it is to find out why it is negative and how we can expand it and make it open to everybody and take out the fear that people like me have, and have them talk and write about everything that they think is the most frightening thing. And I think if this work continues, that will happen.

DANA: We should recognize the limits of it and appreciate —

SIMA: Yeah, and open it up more.

DOROTHY: That's why we're asking the question, because we feel like, yes, it's messy, there's all sorts of differences, yes, we can't provide everything that's necessary, but how do we open it up? That's what this book is about.

MARIA: And getting that small bit of you at least is a start.

CHRISTIE: As long as we acknowledge the power imbalance which exists everywhere, depending on our race and our class and our age and our income level and our gender and our sexual orientation. So many things.

If we never communicated with each other until there was a totally equal power balance, we wouldn't have anybody to talk to or write to. We're all coming from totally different places and spaces. So, we're always censoring ourselves, in one way and another. So it's a valid criticism that that occurs, but I don't think that makes it a reason not to do the journals.

DOROTHY: *Well, we just had one more major question, which is, what do you think about contributing to this book?*

GUNNEL: All right! I'm famous!

CHRISTIE: I'm also looking forward to getting to read everyone else's journal. You don't get to do that very often.

MARIA: In the entry I put in I was talking about the shame, releasing it, and it's not released yet and when this is published the same things will run through my mind, "Oh, my mom"... But I like that and I like the challenges and confronting the risk again.

DAPHNE: I wanted more space! And my second response is, yeah, stuff that my mother would read, because I used the "f" word, a bad word [laughter]. It's just very exciting.

GUNNEL: I was actually the happiest with this entry that you will be using. But it reminds me of another thing I wrote once about art. Usually we think art is [done by] somebody who's paid to do it. When I was writing this, I didn't know what was going to happen with it. I mean, here I am, average person, and this is what's going to be put out and read. This is what the journal writing was all about, that what I write is important, and the person that reads the page is important.

LAURA: I was really awed by the wisdom of all those ordinary women and grateful to have been able to read what they had to say [when you showed us the manuscript]. I think the fact that these are not eminent scholars, or well-known activists, but just us, is a wonderful reminder that in each other we have vast, important resources.

SIMA: I used to think of writing as magic, by fictional characters that probably don't exist. I always had great respect for those who write and whose writing is published, but when I thought of giving my journals to be published I really didn't take it seriously, I mean published! But now that I saw it here, "Wow, I am fictional now." I'm that character now. I really look forward to reading the whole thing.

DOROTHY: I talked to somebody after the meeting last night. She was saying, "Oh, why did you have to pick those pieces?" and I think that's true, that no matter what we put in, you might feel that way. 'Cause you've moved on, you're somewhere else. But what we wanted to show was the process of creation, that you don't come out with some polished piece. What I love about these pieces is that they are so raw and so real at the same time. There's real kernels of happiness and joy and pain and analytical insight and truth and all of that in there. It's not a book of finished poems; they're journals, and there's beauty in that form.

CHRISTIE: One of the pieces I put in is how I was feeling about my sister-in-law, and my other brother's girlfriend, both pregnant, and I had an abortion. My whole family was so excited about the new babies in the family, and they didn't know that I'd had an abortion, and I was going through all kinds of emotional turmoil over that. I had forgotten which journal entries I'd put in and [now] my sister-in-law's had her second baby recently and my brother phoned tonight to tell me they're expecting their second baby. So it's like two years later, they're each having another baby, and it's really okay now; it's just teaching me how that feels.

ELAINE: Usually in finished work you never see the process. You never learn how the writer thought those thoughts through. So that's why I like even the beginnings, although they're slow and stuff, 'cause it's like this person goes, "Oh, it's time to write in my journal and I have nothing to write about." Then one thought twigs to another thought, and that thought twigs to another thought,...

LEAH MINUK: I'm so excited. As I said when I came in here, this for me is really profound because I want to write, and I've never had the confidence, or the permission, the lack of shame, to write. It may not be the greatest thing I ever write, but it will be in print, and it will be there, and it's like a stepping stone. So for me this a real gift, and not what I expected. So could I change my piece quick?

CONTRIBUTORS' NOTES

MAUREEN D. AFFLECK: I am currently attending law school and hope to work in the area of women's rights.

VARNEY ALLIS is over forty and shares the parenting of her two boys with their father. It was about a year after Women's Studies that she had the courage to leave the marriage and set up a separate household. She loves her full-time job as a teacher, but often thinks about how to get (beg, borrow or steal?) more time for writing.

JULIE ELISE ARCHER: I was born in Vancouver a year after my parents came to Canada, but I have been to Ireland many times, with my family when I was a kid and more recently with my partner, Carla. In between trips I work at a bookstore and live with Carla and our cats, Emma and Max.

BAD GIRL LIAR: These were names used to silence me. I come from a normal home with a lot of love. I also come from a home that is vested in strict gender roles, religious dogma, and traditional childrearing practices. As I look around my culture, I see that normal does not equal healthy or ideal.

MARIA LISE BAILEY: Twenty-three-year-old student working towards a Master's in Social Work and developing greater love, power and wisdom.

LIDWINA BAUTISTA: I am a full-time mother of three teenagers, a full-time health-care worker and, in my spare time, I take courses to get away and challenge myself.

BONNIE: I returned to school at the age of thirty-eight with a grade 7 education and a very low self-esteem. I am presently working as a social worker and family violence counsellor for my community. Please do not let your limited education or age hold you back from fulfilling your dreams.

THEA BOWERING: To love is to make up the other
and the biggest abuse to the loving lover
is to refuse to imagine her/him
I am thankful to those who have imagined me
I am still in love with those who have imagined me
I am still imagining.

DAPHNE BOXILL: Twenty-seven, black and ... well, you know.

B.J. is a woman in transition, searching for a meaningful existence.

MORGAN BRAYTON: After dropping out of high school I went to work as a film and television actress/waitress. My experiences as both drove me first to drink and then to feminism. I decided to go to college and am now completing my diploma in Women's Studies with plans to attend university and become a filmmaker. I suppose I am engaged in the same struggles as many women: struggling to find the balance between taking care of others and taking care of myself. I have this revolutionary notion that the two are not mutually exclusive.

DEBBRA BROWN: Fairly certain she was sent to the wrong planet, Debbra struggles to fully experience life by living honestly beyond the confines of a mainstream existence. Along her journey she has found great comfort from the ocean's breeze, the words of children and the strength of trees.

MICHELLE CANNON-BURLEY: I am a twenty-nine-year-old heterosexual survivor of family abuse and violence. Although I have never had to endure an abortion, I have been faced with deciding what I might do should the need arise. I strongly believe in the family with children if they are going to be loved and cared for in a healthy manner, not forced on an unwanting woman.

JENNIFER CONROY is at present studying sociology and English at SFU. Between papers, she reads avidly, writes poetry and drinks a lot of coffee.

ELAINE DORNAN: I am a poverty-class white woman who is somewhat happily absorbed in the juggle of solo-parenting, sporadic paid employment, some volunteer work and full-time schooling. After twenty-six years of street life I went back to school at age thirty-eight. I am deeply and personally interested in issues of class, race, sexuality, age and power.

KAREN EGGER: Thirty-eight years old, white, lesbian mother of one son, an Early-Childhood educator, trying to do my part to heal myself and the earth. Writing a journal within Women's Studies was a wonderful opportunity for me to explore issues and ideas in my life.

GINA MARINA CIFUENTES FAENA: "Tell us another story, Mama," scream the kids in the car. "No, I'm tired." "Please, come on, just one more, I know, the one about Cathy Hope and how she got her leg stuck." "Yeah, that one." Lost in school, papers due, money, work, supper, traffic, the Journal Project, my entries about identity, motherhood, words that paint pictures, for me and others. "Mama, Mama, come on, are you listening?"

"What, yeah, O.K." I give in, I consent, because for no matter what reasons, stories, our stories are important. "Well, one day at recess ..."

CORAL GALLAGHER: Most importantly — a mother, wife, sister and friend — who takes these roles seriously. My entries reflect the challenges that my personal relationships present and the enjoyment I receive from them.

TERRY GIBSON is a UBC student and Vancouver activist. She rolls her eyes now at her continued use of feminist clichés and feels "empowered" by telling her story.

LAURA GLOMBA: The Journal Project allowed me as a mother and a student to explore the thoughts and emotions that surfaced during class.

SUHASINE SARA PAGH HANSEN: I am a twenty-three-year-old student working on my Bachelor of Fine Arts at Emily Carr College of Art and Design. I owe my insights and my will to succeed in the Fine Arts to my brother, Jonathan Morner, who passed away May 1993, at the age of twelve, after a long six years of struggling with cancer. Thank you, Jonathan, for showing me the way.

TRACEY HERBERT: What I want people to know about me and my writing. I am a Shuswap womyn from Bonaparte Indian Band. My healing journey has lead me home to my grandparents and the special place where I grew up in the presence of my ancestors, We wisk an. The two journal entries in this book reflect my impatience with male-dominated society and my dreams for a better place for myself, my family and Indian people.

PAT J.: Family Counsellor. I have been studying for the past five years. I have not worked in any job as yet but hopefully in the coming new years I'll have a brighter future. I am a single parent and have a sixteen-year-old daughter, who's also struggling with life.

JENNIFER KEANE: Jennifer's goal upon returning to school — to complete a master's degree in Counselling Psychology — is within sight. She will specialize in women's issues, particularly in the area of eating disorders.

DOROTHY KIDD: When I am not responding to the journals of Women's Studies students, I keep a journal of my own everyday activities and reflections as a white lesbian feminist mediapunk and sometime teacher of alternative and mainstream Communications.

PEARL KIRBY: I am currently a student at Simon Fraser University. I have a minor in Women's Studies and am hoping for a degree in Film. I "came out" as a writer in my Women's Studies classes because of the journal assignments. I have written articles for *Kinesis*, I won a prize for best fiction in *West 49th Avenue* magazine and I am now working on my first novel.

LESLIE RENE LO: was born in Vancouver and was raised by her mother, a second generation Chinese Canadian who struggled with the complexities of an era unable to accommodate the worlds between gender and race. Leslie acknowledges her mother as one of the countless sentinels who have contributed to the language of difference, a language she now enjoys sharing with the daughters and sons of parents who likewise have set back the parameters of ignorance.

JACKIE LYNNE: I hope my readers will find value in my work.

PATI MATHIAS: Now happily back in the Okanagan hinterlands, I work at developing our health-care consulting business, gardening, community activism, learning the writer's craft, perpetual renovation and "just getting on with it."

LEAH MEREDITH: Hi! I am an SFU student and part-time hockey dyke. I hope to finish a degree in Counselling Psychology before escaping into the woods with my partner, our cats and a few good books.

LAURA MERVYN: At thirty-eight, who I am continues to emerge from the layers of who I was taught I should be. I am white, lesbian, feminist, mother, sister, daughter and sometimes lover. I continue to learn and unlearn, grow and resist.

LEAH MINUK: I am a mother, a lesbian, a student, a feminist; a lover of silence and a believer in the power of words, and the freedom to voice them. I thank Sophia for any bit of wisdom found in the words I write.

KASTHURI MOODLEY-ISMAIL: Kay is a South African mother and full-time student who has experienced Canadian culture and lifestyle as very challenging.

PATTY MOORE: is particularly happy to be a mother and an instructor of Women's Studies and at the same time is drawn to red convertibles heading out of town.

JEAN MORAN: I still struggle with issues of control, depression, obesity, trust, self-esteem, absence of a meaningful social life, and tardiness. Thankfully, enough small victories have been realized over the last three years that my belief in myself has been vastly strengthened and practically all my twitches have disappeared.

GLORIA MURRAY: Throughout my life I have kept a journal (diary), sometimes writing consistently for several months, sometimes not writing for a year or two. It relaxes me and connects me to myself.

IRIS FABIOLA NAGUIB: I am biracial, I am a woman, I am a survivor, I am
_____ (not ready to say ...), I am a loner, a meditator and a lover of
mother earth in all her forms. I am angry, I am passionate, I am a fighter, I
am loved and now I also love myself. I am thirsty, I am tired, I am scared, I
am strong, I am a poet, I am wise, I am a baby, I am a bitch, I am an artist,
I am crazy and sometimes I'm sane, ... but now I try harder to remember
that before I am anything, I am me, ... I am spirit, I am soul, I am, ...

MICHELLE ELIZABETH NEILSON: Women's Studies opened my ears and let
me hear my sisters' stories and realize that their experience really counts,
and so does mine. Taking those classes helped to nourish, foster and
change my political beliefs. Most of all it empowered me, released my creativity and started me on a journey of finding my own voice. I left Langara
in the spring of 1993. I am presently studying acting full-time at Gastown
Actors Studio.

TANIS POOLE: I am a thirty-seven-year-old mother of two. I never dreamt
that Women's Studies would be so fulfilling. It has put me on a wonderful
path. I am currently exploring women's spirituality, opening to the
Goddess in creation. I was not able to celebrate my passage through maid-
enhood. I plan to celebrate mother and crone.

SHERRY PRESTON: Have moved on to Simon Fraser University, where I will
continue to learn about the lives of women.

DANA MAURINE PUTNAM: I am a university student and mother continuing to struggle with the contradictions of being a feminist working for an
alternative future within a system that refuses to change.

GLORIA ELVIRA ROQUE: Born in El Salvador, I came to Canada when I was
twelve years old. I work with the Vancouver Latin American community
and I am currently finishing my Bachelor of Education at SFU. I am a
Salvadorian-Canadian radical woman of colour.

LAURIE SCHUERBEKE: I live in Vancouver with my partner, Daryl. I teach
assault prevention to teens and women. I teach them how to say NO. A
two-letter word goes a far way. I see women of all ages discovering their
power — their full beings — and it reminds me of what i most need to
learn. This is why i am here.

BECCA SHEARS: After my first Women's Studies class at Langara, I got
politically involved with women's issues. Through that empowering experience, I was able to come out as a lesbian and a feminist (with support from
that boyfriend). I am now finishing my last year of university majoring in

Psychology and Women's Studies. I hope to work with women as a counsellor in the future.

Sima: Ten years ago, if someone had asked me who I was, I would have answered Arab-Iranian. A few years later, I felt I was entirely Arab, since I had to qualify my accent and dark skin, even to Iranians. Taking first-year Women's Studies made me realize that I belonged to a bigger camp, that of women of colour. Now I identify myself as feminist, third-year linguistics major at Simon Fraser University, Vancouverite and woman of colour.

Kate Slaney: At the time I wrote these journal entries I was in my first year of university. I have since graduated with a BA, major — Psychology, minor — Women's Studies. I feel encouraged by the fact that I'm still struggling with where my place, as a feminist, is — encouraged because I believe that the wisdom is gained in the process of the struggle and not in its resolution.

Zara Suleman: As a twenty-something, South Asian feminist, artist, cultural activist and rape crisis counsellor I have found that the work and interests I embraced in Langara Women's Studies continue to be the focus of my research. The challenge exists for all women to reclaim our stories and our experiences. Journal writing has been the site for much of the power and strength in myself and my identity!

Jessie Sutherland: Jessie has moved on in more ways than one. I have journalled and journeyed my way to Montreal and delight in dance, friends, learning and hanging out in cafes. Thanks to Patty Moore for encouraging me to trust my own voice; transforming it from a squeak to a boom!

Margaret Sutherland: I am a Vancouver administrative assistant by day, and a single parent of two. I like used bookstores, South Asian food and political gossip, and have a late-night passion for nineteenth-century "ladies'" novels and chocolate, best enjoyed together.

Jane Swann: I am now twenty-five years old and my son is seven. Many of my views have changed since Women's Studies, however, the course has heavily influenced the direction of my studies. I am currently finishing my Sociology degree and live in Kelowna with my son and girlfriend.

Stacy Tatum: Always in process. Currently working towards inner peace and empowerment through music, writing and yoga. Becoming whole again.

Gunnel Tesfa: I immigrated to Canada from Germany in 1989, and I am currently living with my husband in Vancouver, BC. This summer, I will be graduating from UBC with a master's in Social Work. My commitment to working with and for women has greatly been inspired by my first Women's Studies course at VCC, Langara, and other Women's Studies courses ever since.

MIA TREMBLAY: Lesbian feminist creating!

[Editors' note: Most of Mia's illustrations used in this book came from her Women's Studies journals]

DARCIAN WELYCHENKO: I was born in Winnipeg in 1966. I have recently graduated from SFU and am once again waitressing.

CHRISTIE WOODIN: Born and raised in East Van, Christie's story includes a program in Human Services, travel, a great five-year relationship, extensive work in the school system as a community builder, as well as Women's Studies. Taking a break from work, school and long-term relationships, she is currently on her own in India, more alive and excited about life than ever. A radical feminist, bisexual, politically active, confused and curious individual, she is terrified at having folks read her unedited journal entries, but can't wait to read the others!

BIBLIOGRAPHY

Arat-Koc, Sedef. "Immigration Policies, Migrant and Domestic Workers and Definitions of Citizenship in Canada." In *Deconstructing a Nation: Immigration, Multiculturalism and Racism in the 90's in Canada,* ed. Vic Satzewich. Halifax: Fernwood Publishing, 1992.

Arat-Koc, Sedef. "In the Privacy of Our Own Homes: Foreign Domestic Workers as Solution to the Crisis of the Domestic Sphere in Canada." In *Feminism in Action: Studies in Political Economy,* eds. Patricia Connelly and Pat Armstrong. Toronto: Canadian Scholars Press, 1992.

Bell, Elouise M. "Telling One's Story: Women's Journals Then and Now." In *Women's Personal Narratives: Essays in Criticism and Pedagogy,* eds. Lenore Hoffman and Margo Culley. New York: The Modern Language Association of America, 1985.

Berry, Ellen and Elizabeth Black. "The Integrative Learning Journal" (or, "Getting beyond 'True Confessions' and 'Cold Knowledge'") *Women's Studies Quarterly* 21, no. 3-4 (Fall/Winter 1993): 88-93.

Chrystos. "For Sharon Graves." In *Not Vanishing.* Vancouver: Press Gang Publishers, 1988.

Dworkin, Andrea. *Woman Hating.* New York: Dutton, 1974.

Fulton, Keith Louise. "Journalling Women: The Authentic Voice and Intellectual Cross-Dressing." In *A Reader in Feminist Ethics,* ed. Debra Shogan. Toronto: Canadian Scholar's Press, 1992.

Fulwiler, Toby, ed. *The Journal Book.* Portsmouth, New Hampshire: Boynton Cook, 1987.

Gregory, Deborah. "From Where I Stand: A Case for Feminist Bisexuality." In *Sex and Love: New Thoughts on Old Contradictions,* eds. Sue Cartledge and Joanna Ryan. London: Women's Press, 1983.

Hoffman, Lenore and Margo Culley, eds. *Women's Personal Narratives: Essays in Criticism and Pedagogy.* New York: The Modern Language Association of America, 1985.

hooks, bell. (1989) "Writing from the Darkness." *Writing and Well-Being* (a special issue of *TriQuarterly* magazine edited by Reginald Gibbons and Susan Hahn) 75 (Spring-Summer 1989): 71-77.

————. *Black Looks: Race and Representation.* Toronto: Between the Lines, 1992.

————. "Eros, Eroticism and the Pedagogical Process." *Cultural Studies* 7, no.1 (January 1993): 59-63.

Hughes, Nym. "Why I Can't Write about Class." *Fireweed: A Feminist Quarterly,* no. 25 (July 1987): 21-24.

Jeffereys, Sheila. "Pornography." In *Anticlimax: A Feminist Investigation of Sexual Murder.* London: Women's Press, 1990.

Kelly, Liz. "Sexual Violence as a Continuum." Adapted from a paper presented by Liz Kelly at The National Coalition against Sexual Assault Conference in Great Britain, July 1986. [Although we cannot find the publishing source for this work, we believe "Sexual Violence as a Continuum" is the background research for a book by Kelly entitled *Surviving Sexual Violence,* Cambridge: Polity Press, 1988. On the last page of "Sexual Violence as a Continuum" Liz Kelly gives her address for anyone requesting bibliographic details: Liz Kelly, 47 Wellington Road, Norwich, Norfolk, Great Britain. However, this address may be out of date.

Laurence, Margaret. *The Stone Angel.* Toronto: McClelland and Stewart, 1964.

Lee, C. Allyson. "Letter to My Mother." *Awakening Thunder: Asian Canadian Women — Fireweed: A Feminist Quarterly,* no. 30 (Spring 1990): 91-93.

Levine, Helen. "Swimming Upstream: Reflections of a Feminist at 66." In *Living the Changes,* ed. Joan Turner. Winnipeg: University of Manitoba Press, 1990.

McCannell, Kathryn F. and Barbara M. Herringer. "Changing Terms of Endearment: Women and Families." In *Living the Changes,* ed. Joan Turner. Winnipeg: University of Manitoba Press, 1990.

Martin, Jennifer (playwright). "Tales from a Broken Heart." Play performed at Vancouver Women in View Festival, 1991.

Paredes, Milagros. "From the Inside Out." *Fireweed: A Feminist Quarterly,* no. 30 (Spring 1990): 77-81.

Piercy, Marge. "For Strong Women." In *The Moon Is Always Female.* New York: Knopf, 1980.

Rich, Adrienne. "Compulsory Heterosexuality and Lesbian Existence." *Signs: A Journal of Women in Society* 5, no. 4 (Summer 1980): 62-91.

Ruth, Sheila. "The Naming of Women." In *Issues in Feminism: An Introduction to Women's Studies*, ed. Sheila Ruth. Mountain View, California: Mayfield, 1990.

Schaef, Anne Wilson. *Women's Reality: An Emerging Female System in a White Male Society*. San Francisco: Harper and Row, 1985.

Steinem, Gloria. *Revolution from Within: A Book of Self-Esteem*. Boston: Little, Brown, 1992.

Sternbach, Nancy Saporta. "Re-membering the Dead: Latin American Women's 'Testimonial' Discourse." *Latin American Perspectives* 18, no. 3 (Summer 1991): 91-102.

Sullivan, Anne McCrary. "Liberating the Urge to Write: From Classroom Journals to Lifelong Writing." *English Journal* 78 (November 1989): 55-61.

Szekely, Eva. *Never Too Thin*. Toronto: Women's Press, 1988.

Wagner, Jane. *Search for Signs of Intelligent Life in the Universe*. New York: Harper and Row, 1986.

Waugh, Susan. "Women's Shorter Autobiographical Writings: Expression, Identity and Form." In *Women's Personal Narratives: Essays in Criticism and Pedagogy*, eds. Lenore Hoffman and Margo Culley. New York: The Modern Language Association of America, 1985.

Woolf, Virginia. *A Room of One's Own*. Penguin: London, 1945.

Wollman-Bonilla, Julie E. "Reading Journals: Invitations to Participate in Literature." *The Reading Teacher* 43 (November 1989): 112-20.

Zacharias, Martha E. "The Relationship between Journal Writing in Education and Thinking Processes: What Educators Say about It." *Education* 112, no. 2 (Winter 1991): 265-70.

FILMS

A Class Divided. Prod. and dir. William Peters. 58 min. Washington, DC: PBS, 1985. Videocassette.

After the Montreal Massacre. Prod. Nicole Huber. Dir. Gerry Rogers. 28 min. National Film Board of Canada and Canadian Broadcasting Corporation, 1989. Videocassette.

The Diviners. Prods. Kim Todd and Derek Mazur. Dir. Anne Wheeler. 117 min. Atlantis Films, 1992. Videocassette.

Margaret Laurence: First Lady of Manawaka. Prod. William Weinteraub. Dir. Robert Duncan. 52:52 min. NFB, 1978. Videocassette.

Not a Love Story: a Film About Pornography. Prod. Dorothy Todd Henaut. Dir. Bonnie Sherri Klein. 69 min. NFB, Studio D, 1981. Videocassette.

Sandra's Garden. Prod. Joe MacDonald. Dir. Bonnie Dickie. 34 min. NFB, 1990. Videocassette.

Sisters in the Struggle. Dir. Dionne Brand. Dir. and prod. Ginny Stikeman. 49 min. NFB, Studio D, 1990.

Sitting in Limbo. Prod. David Wilson. Dir. John N. Smith. 95:19 min. NFB, 1986. Videocassette.

Free from retribution
eve grows her own apple tree.